TEECHERS LEAVERS 22

by John Godber

SAMUEL FRENCH

Copyright © 2023 by John Godber
All Rights Reserved
Original *TEECHERS* Text Copyright © 1989 by John Godber

TEECHERS LEAVERS 22 is fully protected under the copyright laws of the British Commonwealth, including Canada, the United States of America, and all other countries of the Copyright Union. All rights, including professional and amateur stage productions, recitation, lecturing, public reading, motion picture, radio broadcasting, television, online/digital production, and the rights of translation into foreign languages are strictly reserved.

ISBN 978-0-573-00007-2

concordtheatricals.co.uk
concordtheatricals.com

FOR AMATEUR PRODUCTION ENQUIRIES

UNITED KINGDOM AND WORLD
EXCLUDING NORTH AMERICA
licensing@concordtheatricals.co.uk
020-7054-7298

Each title is subject to availability from Concord Theatricals, depending upon country of performance.

CAUTION: Professional and amateur producers are hereby warned that *TEECHERS LEAVERS 22* is subject to a licensing fee. The purchase, renting, lending or use of this book does not constitute a licence to perform this title(s), which licence must be obtained from the appropriate agent prior to any performance. Performance of this title(s) without a licence is a violation of copyright law and may subject the producer and/or presenter of such performances to penalties. Both amateurs and professionals considering a production are strongly advised to apply to the appropriate agent before starting rehearsals, advertising, or booking a theatre. A licensing fee must be paid whether the title is presented for charity or gain and whether or not admission is charged.

This work is published by Samuel French, an imprint of Concord Theatricals Ltd.

The Professional Rights in this play are controlled by Alan Brodie Representation.

No one shall make any changes in this title for the purpose of production. No part of this book may be reproduced, stored in a retrieval system, scanned, uploaded, or transmitted in any form, by any means, now known or yet to be invented, including mechanical, electronic, digital, photocopying, recording, videotaping, or otherwise, without the prior written permission of the publisher. No one shall share this title, or part of this title, to any social media or file hosting websites.

The moral right of John Godber to be identified as author of this work has been asserted in accordance with Section 77 of the Copyright, Designs and Patents Act 1988.

USE OF COPYRIGHTED MUSIC

A licence issued by Concord Theatricals to perform this play does not include permission to use the incidental music specified in this publication. In the United Kingdom: Where the place of performance is already licensed by the PERFORMING RIGHT SOCIETY (PRS) a return of the music used must be made to them. If the place of performance is not so licensed then application should be made to PRS for Music (www.prsformusic.com). A separate and additional licence from PHONOGRAPHIC PERFORMANCE LTD (www.ppluk.com) may be needed whenever commercial recordings are used. Outside the United Kingdom: Please contact the appropriate music licensing authority in your territory for the rights to any incidental music.

USE OF COPYRIGHTED THIRD-PARTY MATERIALS

Licensees are solely responsible for obtaining formal written permission from copyright owners to use copyrighted third-party materials (e.g., artworks, logos) in the performance of this play and are strongly cautioned to do so. If no such permission is obtained by the licensee, then the licensee must use only original materials that the licensee owns and controls. Licensees are solely responsible and liable for clearances of all third-party copyrighted materials, and shall indemnify the copyright owners of the play(s) and their licensing agent, Concord Theatricals Ltd., against any costs, expenses, losses and liabilities arising from the use of such copyrighted third-party materials by licensees.

IMPORTANT BILLING AND CREDIT REQUIREMENTS

If you have obtained performance rights to this title, please refer to your licensing agreement for important billing and credit requirements.

TEECHERS LEAVERS 22 was a co-production with Hull Truck Theatre as part of their 50th anniversary celebrations, John Godber re-imagined his iconic play for the leavers of 2022. The performance was directed by Mark Babych. The cast was as follows:

SALTY . . . . Levi Payne
GAIL. . . . . Purvi Parmar
HOBBY. . . . . .Martha Godber

Original and West End productions directed by John Godber.

CHARACTERS

SALTY – A school-student bright and fresh-faced, rather dirty in appearance. Plays **TEACHER A**, **MRS PARRY**, **MR JONES**, **PETE SAXON**, **OGGY**, **BARRY**, **RON**, **DR BASFORD DEANIE**, and **MR CLIFTON**.

GAIL – Loud-mouthed and bossy, attractive and full of enthusiasm. Plays **TEACHER B**, **MS WHITHAM**, **OGGY**, **DR BASFORD**, **MR HATTON**, **JACKIE PRIME**, **PIGGY**, **DENNIS**, **DOUG**, and **MRS COATES**.

HOBBY – Hard. Should be large, must be bigger than the other two. She is doing the play despite herself. Plays **MS NIXON** and **MRS PARRY**.

MS NIXON – New drama teacher, young and casual.

MRS PARRY – The Executive Head, large and loud, a real eccentric.

DR BASFORD – The Deputy Head, strict but good, a nasty piece of work.

MISS PRIME – PE mistress.

MS WHITHAM – A fussy and hopeless teacher, desperate to leave.

MS JONES – A moaner, rather fat, someone who wants to leave but no one will employ.

DEANIE – A teacher.

DOUG – Site Staff, a miserable man, he hates kids and drama.

OGGY – The cock of the school, looks much older than he actually is, the school bully in a modern age.

PETE SAXON – A large, frightening youth with tattoos, appears foolish.

MR FISHER – Head of PE.

BARRY WOBSCHALL – A small boy who never brings his PE kit.

PIGGY PATTERSON – A boy who is always telling on others, he always runs to his lessons.

RON – A boy who never does PE.

MR HATTON – Helps with the youth club dance.

DENNIS – Oggy's side-kick.

MRS COATES – Head Mistress at Saint George's.

MR CLIFTON – Head of Governors at Saint George's.

SETTING

The action takes place in a comprehensive school hall.

TIME

The present.

AUTHOR'S NOTES

Teechers Leavers 22 was designed to be played by three actors, multi-role playing twenty other parts in a play-within-a-play format. Everything about the production was reduced to the basic essentials: actors, stage, audience. I wanted to produce a play that relied on the same bare essentials that a drama teacher might have in school: kids (actors), a few chairs and desks (the set), and an audience. With these basic ingredients anything can happen in a drama lesson; indeed, the characters in *Teechers Leavers 22* illustrate that once talent has been tapped in school the result is often staggering. Multi-role playing is also, it must be said, an economic as well as artistic consideration. Maybe if I had twenty actors at my disposal I would have produced a different play? In this version of the play the twenty multi-roled parts have been listed in order that twenty actors (kids) could perform the play if so desired. However the play is performed, actors or students, it is important to remember that *Teechers Leavers 22* is a comedy, a comedy which illustrates many anxieties in education today. Comedies must primarily be funny, here is a comedy, I think, which is also deadly serious.

THE SET

Nothing is required in the way of a set except for three plastic briefcases, old newspapers for the staff-room scenes, a broom for Doug, and two chairs and two open-top desks for the various other settings, all of which should be easily obtained in school. When produced by three actors, character differentiation is helped by the use of funny noses (which the kids would have bought cheaply from W. H. Smith's). Clearly when the play is produced with a larger cast a proportional increase in props is to be expected.

THE MUSIC

The author recommends that any incidental music in the play be contemporary chart music. Please contact PRS to ascertain the music publisher and contact such music publisher to license or acquire permission for performance of any songs. For further information, please see the Use of Copyrighted Music note on page iii.

TEECHERS LEAVERS 22

When I wrote the original *Teechers* back in the early 1980s I had no idea that it would be so enduring, or that its themes would still be relevant almost forty years later. I had always wanted to be a drama teacher, discovering drama in a state secondary school was a revelation for me, and I have two great drama teachers to thank for that.

You might have thought that drama would be widely accepted in school as a core subject and a highly regarded area of investigation, and yet, it saddens me to report, that in some secondary schools drama has less status now than it did when I was teaching back in 1983.

For anyone who understands the central importance of drama in the curriculum as both a subject and a tool for educational research, not to mention it's human aspects in the round, the absence of drama for all in our schools is an outrage in my view.

Those of us who have seen first hand how it can engage, stimulate, grow, challenge and develop young people will stand aghast as we contemplate a Government who are promoting maths to be studied until students are eighteen. It's not that I'm bad at maths, I'm actually rather good; but it undoubtedly demonstrates a clear lack of knowledge about the importance of the person in the educational process, for as the late lamented Sir Ken Robinson observed two decades ago: we have to educate the whole person, not just that bit above the neck! For me that means developing empathy, sensitivity, imagination, mutual understanding and cooperation, in short the things that make us connect as humans beings. Underneath the lunacy and comedy in Teechers the message is clear!

John Godber OBE
Hull. 2023

ACT ONE

(A comprehensive school hall 2022.)

*(A wooden stage. There are two old wooden double desks upstage. Upstage right is an old locker with a school broom leaning against it. Downstage centre is a chair; left and right two single desks and chairs angled downstage, and three bags. A satchel, plastic bags and sports bags are near the chairs and desks. They belong to **SALTY**, **GAIL** and **HOBBY** respectively. The students wear a variation of the school uniform, all have seen better days. **HOBBY**'s trousers are slightly too short and she wears boots which make her taller, even though she is a unit already. She is a hard-faced, frightening girl. **SALTY** is cheeky and instantly likeable a powder keg of energy. **GAIL** is impish and lively, likeable and unreliable. The shirts they wear are worn and old, blue ties with a stripe are worn in various styles. with blue blazers and a poorly design school badge. Despite the uniformity it is clear these students are low on financial support. Slowly **SALTY**, **GAIL** and **HOBBY** enter, and look at the audience, they have Covid-19 masks which hang from their chins. As the play begins the masks get secreted in to their pockets. They are nervously excited, and eyeball the audience; which is the entire school, they acknowledge friends and staff. There is a tense silence before they start.)*

SALTY. All right?

GAIL. Look at 'em!

SALTY. Are you nervous?

HOBBY. We are!

> *(They are nervously enjoying their power.)*

SALTY. Been an odd two years!

GAIL. Mrs Hudson's, there look!

SALTY. All right Mrs Hudson?

> *(They wave at the audience.)*

HOBBY. Alright Dr Bishop?

SALTY. Look at his face!

GAIL. All right, Mrs Weaver?

> *(A beat.)*

HOBBY. Can't believe t' whole schools looking at us!

> *(A beat.)*

SALTY. Can't believe we're not doing it on Zoom!

GAIL. I bet you wish we were don't you Miss?

HOBBY. I don't, I want to do it!

> *(**GAIL** is self deprecating.)*

GAIL. You've got to suffer this in-person!

> *(A beat.)*

SALTY. I've always wanted to be on this stage. I've always wanted to come up here and say, "School's shit." I bet you all have. Whenever I see Mrs Hudson come up here to talk about Social Responsibility or being a good Samaritan or Safe-Guarding, I think about that. Cos really Mrs Hudson would like to come up here and say, "Shit to the lot o' you!"

GAIL. Are we doing it then?

SALTY. It's like when she gets you in her office, all neat and smelling of perfume and she says, "You don't come to school to fool around, to waste your time. We treat you like young adults and we expect you to behave accordingly. I don't think that writing silly comments on a wall is a mature thing to do."

HOBBY. That's good that.

SALTY. Yeh, but really she wants to say, "Hey Salty, pack all this graffiti in, it's getting on my tits."

GAIL. Look at 'em just looking!

SALTY. Anyway why am I bothered, this is it. No more school, after today mate!

HOBBY. It's college for us!

GAIL. No more Miss Jubb shouting like you're deaf as a post, "Gail Saunders how dare you belch in front of me." Didn't know it was your turn…

HOBBY. Funny!

SALTY. No more full school assemblies sat on the cold floor of the sports hall freezing your arse off!

GAIL. No more running round t' school field, and cold showers and people saying; it's good for you.

HOBBY. No more Zooming!

GAIL. No more scenes in the changing rooms where you daren't get changed because you wear a vest and everyone else has got a bra…

HOBBY. Mind you I wasn't on Zoom half the time, turned it off.

GAIL. No more teachers with beards and hush puppies.

SALTY. No more teachers, who say "I'm just like you"!

HOBBY. That's you Sir!!

GAIL. No more having to run the fifteen hundred metres with a heart condition.

SALTY. No more.

HOBBY. Cos today we're off.

GAIL. Let's start!

SALTY. Hang on, before we start, we want to <u>thank</u> Ms Nixon, our drama teacher. Before she came here three years ago, we weren't really interested in drama. And we know that she's been offered a job at a better school…But before Miss came here, the teachers had given us up for dead…We were average.

HOBBY. Yes they said; I was average, she opens her book well, and likes a warm room!

GAIL. They never said that!

HOBBY. They did!

SALTY. Well I don't feel average today, I feel like a boss… thanks to Miss.

HOBBY. I was told not to do drama, they said it was a waste of an option, and now I've helped put this together!

SALTY. This is what we did for our B.Tech performance on Zoom, and it includes Brechtian techniques, and physical theatre!

GAIL. Yes, but we've adapted.

HOBBY. First time we've done it in front of real people!

GAIL. That's made them nervous!

SALTY. A lot of the stuff in it was told to us by Miss over the last three years.

HOBBY. So blame her!

GAIL. And even though you might not like it, everything what happens in the play is based on truth

HOBBY. But the names and the faces have been changed.

GAIL. To protect the innocent.

SALTY. But you know who you are!

GAIL. We're going to take you to Whitewall Academy. It's a comprehensive somewhere in the north of England…

HOBBY. Near Hull!

GAIL. It's in Hull actually!

HOBBY. On a big estate!

GAIL. And they're expecting a new drama teacher to arrive…

HOBBY. …Coz the other one had a breakdown! There's seventeen hundred kids at Whitewall and it's got Serious Weaknesses!

GAIL. And it nearly failed it's Ofsted!

HOBBY. Which means that it's got issues right.

SALTY. All we want you to do is use your imagination because there's only three of us, and we all have to play different characters…

HOBBY. And narrators.

SALTY. And narrators.

HOBBY. So you'll have to concentrate…

SALTY. Oh yeh, you'll have to concentrate…

GAIL. Say the title Salty!

SALTY. Oh shit, yeh… And it's called *Teechers* –

GAIL. – *Leavers 22, Scenes from our school*!

HOBBY. Coz that's what it is, right!

(LX.)

(A sudden burst of music. They become **TEACHERS**, with briefcases and files, There is a physicality to their storytelling which belies their actual abilities. Three overhead spots pick them out across the centre of the stage. The lyric nature of the dialogue gives them a stylish physical manner through their story telling. Music fades.)*

HOBBY. Arrive first thing…

GAIL. Into the car park…

HOBBY. Through the gates…

SALTY. Find your spot…

GAIL. Mine's gone!

SALTY. Take another!

HOBBY. Quarter to eight on the dot!

SALTY. Kids, cars, chaos!

HOBBY. Steel fencing at every turn!

GAIL. Across the road!

HOBBY. Houses boarded!

SALTY. They're being replaced!

GAIL. It's taking time!

SALTY. With levelling up

HOBBY. It'll all be fine!

---

* A licence to produce *Teechers Leavers 22* does not include a performance licence for any third-party or copyrighted music. Licensees should create an original composition or use music in the public domain. For further information, please see the Music and Third-Party Materials Use Note on page iii.

SALTY. Into reception!

GAIL. Signing in!

SALTY. Photo done!

HOBBY. Lanyard on!

GAIL. Sanitise!

ALL. Sanitise!

SALTY. To the left!

GAIL. To the right!

HOBBY. Put your mask on!

ALL. Sanitise!

SALTY. To the left!

GAIL. To the right!

HOBBY. Put your mask on!

ALL. Sanitise!

> *(The three actors move across the stage chasing their spotlight positions as they do the personify various staff who are now in the large corridors of the school. They essentially switch overhead spots.)*

GAIL. Morning.

HOBBY. Morning.

SALTY. Morning.

HOBBY. Morning.

GAIL. Morning.

PARRY. Stop running Simon Patterson.

TEACHER A. Morning Olly.

PARRY. Morning, Mike.

TEACHER B. Morning, Dr. Basford.

ALL. Morning, Mrs Parry…

PARRY. Good-morning…

WITHAM. You are chewing, girl, spit it out. Not into her hair, into a bin…

TEACHER B. I don't call that a straight line, do you, Kieren Macheath? No? Neither do I.

PARRY. I know that was the bell, Simon Patterson. The bell is a signal for me to move and not for anyone else.

> (**HOBBY** becomes **MS NIXON**. *She slips on a stylish jackets which will denote when she plays the drama teacher. She slightly adjusts her demeanour of a nervous new teacher who is learning on the job QTS.*)

NIXON. I'm Sharn Nixon the new drama teacher; yes I know it's unbelievable but go with it! And I'm looking for Mrs Parry's office.

SALTY. Up the steps in the nice part of the school, first left.

> (**HOBBY** *exits, to sit upstage.*)

GAIL & SALTY. Mmmmmmmmmmmmm.

GAIL. She doesn't look much like a teacher; looks like somebody who's selling hairspray!

> (**HOBBY** *comes downstage as* **NIXON**.)

NIXON. I knew at my interview that Whitewall had a dodgy reputation and no drama facilities. But I went to a school like this; I'd seen what drama can do! So I made my way up to the Executive Head's office, but she was busy with Dr Basford, of the SLT. That's Senior Learning Team!

> (**GAIL** *dons a facial mask, nose and glasses from a lift-top desk, (which all the cast wear as* **DR BASFORD**) **SALTY** *becomes* **MRS PARRY**, *with the help of a scarf taken from one of the desks.)*
>
> *(LX.)*

BASFORD. I don't believe you're doing this.

PARRY. It's what's best for the Academy, we've got the Primary pupils helping with the chorus, we need to make links with our feeder schools!

BASFORD. After all the work I've put in, now you turn around and tell me that I'm not Koko!

PARRY. Dr. Basford. it's pointless doing *The Mikado* if we don't have the best casting. I'm sure you'll have a great deal of fun in the chorus.

BASFORD. In the chorus with the Primary kids?

PARRY. I'm spinning plates!

BASFORD. Aren't we all?

PARRY. I'm sorry, but I have another appointment!

BASFORD. I wouldn't be seen dead in the bloody chorus!

> (**BASFORD** *replaces his mask in a desk and* **GAIL** *goes upstage to watch.)*

PARRY. Mrs Parry, or should I say Cordelia Parry, BA M.Ed MBA. was a huge attractive woman. She carried herself very well but had awful dress sense, and would often mix pink with yellow. She was of large frame with a voice to match. Ms Nixon? Sharn Nixon?

NIXON. That's right.

PARRY. Hello, nice to see you again. Coffee?

NIXON. Please. Mrs Parry's office was a cavern of theatre posters… She certainly had more than a passing interest.

PARRY. Drama in school, so critical! Ken Robinson, what thinker! This is my all-male production of *The Trojan Women,* and this is me as Ophelia.

NIXON. Behind her head was a photo of a much lither Mrs Parry in an amateur production of *Hamlet.*

PARRY. I'm going to *The Mikado*!

NIXON. *(Audience.)* I knew what she meant. I'd seen it *done* before!

PARRY. Drama is so important, but no one seems to value it anymore, we are so up against it in the state system!

NIXON. Are we?

PARRY. We need funds, we need sponsorship, we need good stories, we need people to want to send their children here. Goodness knows; look where we are!

NIXON. I came from a similar estate!

PARRY. Parent power they call it. We are all consumers now Ms Nixon. A good education is a right not a luxury!

NIXON. Amen to that!

PARRY. And we've got great staff here Sharn, everyone's fighting, but we're led by donkeys in the government who have had a different education all together!

NIXON. Sadly!

PARRY. They haven't got clue what it's really like!

NIXON. Well I'm told empathy…

PARRY. …Empathy! Absolutely, you have to know how much a pint of milk is otherwise we are just patronising do gooders!

NIXON. Forty-nine pence!

PARRY. Sorry?

NIXON. Forty-nine pence…in Tesco's. You might get it cheaper but…

PARRY. Excellent!

NIXON. My Dad was a bus driver… I'm the first generation to go to University!

PARRY. So was I. But the donkeys don't understand that! But what can we do? We fight on, we do what we can!

NIXON. I guess!

PARRY. I knew you'd get it! You see Dr Basford usually takes the lead in our local productions but he was rather tiresome last year in *The Pyjama Game* but we have to compete! Well that's given you something to think about!

NIXON. It certainly has.

PARRY. And so to business.

> (**PARRY** *freezes.*)

NIXON. The meeting went on for another twenty minutes, but I got the message. With another Ofsted coming up the school had got to succeed. Otherwise it'd be a carpet warehouse!

> (**GAIL** *animates.*)

GAIL. But one thing struck her about Mrs Parry. She really did care about the kids at Whitewall.

> (**PARRY** *and* **NIXON** *come downstage and look into the large screen of a computer. LX picks them out.*)

PARRY. As we walked from my office...I wished Sharn all the best with her induction year, and took her towards Dr Basford's room, home of the timetable.

NIXON. The complicated timetable was impossible to fathom. Seventeen digital pages, colour-coded and meticulous, it was certainly a work of art, but impossible to understand. How the frigging hell could any students follow this?

(They are looking at a computer screen.)

PARRY. The nomenclature is fairly straightforward. You will be N.I., Ms Nixon, and drama will be D.R. As you'll be having your lessons in the Main Hall, drama with you in the Main Hall, would read N.I.D.R.M.H. If you have a year three class it could read, N.I.D.R.M.H.I.Y.X. Period one. Fairly simple.

NIXON. How the frigg can <u>anybody</u> follow this?

PARRY. Sorry?

NIXON. Just thinking out loud!

PARRY. If you have any problems at all, don't hesitate, come up and see me straight away. And have a think about *The Mikado*. I know how much the theatre must be in your blood... It could be your big break...

NIXON. So I tentatively said "yes", to a small part in the chorus, and although Mrs Parry was disappointed that I didn't want Koko, she said that I could certainly enjoy my time in Titipu.

(LX.)

*(Music. The scene dissolves and **NIXON** confronts a lost student who is weighed down with bags.)*

LOST. Excuse me, Miss?

NIXON. Eh?

LOST. Miss!

(Addresses the audience.)

NIXON. I'd never been called Miss, before! It threw me, I thought she was talking to someone else!

*(**NIXON** back in the scene.)*

LOST. Miss, I'm lost.

NIXON. Well where should you be?

LOST. I don't know, I can't work it out on my timetable. I'm in tutor group I.D. in Wilberforce Block One. But I'm in teaching group I.Y.Five and I should be in Ghandi block Four, Three.B doing biology. But Three.Y.Y.Six are in there with Mr Dean doing history, he says that I should be in Marvell Three. One. D, but I've been there and the class is empty. Miss, I've been looking for my class for forty minutes.

NIXON. What have you got next?

LOST. PE in the gym.

NIXON. Do you know where that is?

LOST. Yes, miss.

NIXON. Well I suggest that you go and wait there, then at least your class'll find you.

LOST. Right, thanks Miss…

NIXON. Oh, before you go. Have you any idea where Lincoln is?

LOST. Yes its over the bridge!

NIXON. Is there where the other site is?

LOST. Are you looking for the Cathedral?

NIXON. No, I'm looking for Lincoln block, near Plater I.D!

LOST. I'm not sure I'm even at the right school to be honest, good luck!

NIXON. And you!

LOST. *(Tears.)* Urghhhh I don't know where I'm going!

> *(Tears from the young lost student as she dissolves and energy puts them all on desks facing the audience. We are now in the Form Room.)*

HOBBY. When you're a hardnut and fifteen you always have to give teachers a bad time. It's part of the rules of the game…And when there's a new teacher you can be even tougher. In our class we had seen off three tutors in as many weeks.

GAIL. Miss Bell had a breakdown, but they said that she was pregnant.

HOBBY. Then we had a supply teacher who never spoke…

GAIL. And then they sent us a former Copper who'd got shingles!

HOBBY. Yes, he thought he was hard, but he was soft as shit! And he got depression coz he couldn't lay a finger on uz!

GAIL. We used to say anything to him.

HOBBY. And now they've sent us a new teacher. A brand-new, sparkling clean, training on the job teacher!

> *(**HOBBY** becomes the voice of a **TEACHER**.)*

They're only going to be in school for a few more terms…Send them the new girl Nixon…She can cut her teeth on Seven.Y.Y. down in Nine.I.B… It's out of the way, if they eat her or burn her alive we can forget about her.

SALTY. In Seven.Y.Y. there was me, Salty, Gail and Hobby who you know, George Mears – who was about six years old! All right, George?

GAIL. Not bad, Salty, all right…I've been down to our Barney's, he's got a brilliant BMX. We had a great game of rally cross and did a jig saw.

HOBBY. George loved lockdown, he didn't get out of bed for three months!

SALTY. Then there was Dan Scott who never wore decent shoes.

GAIL. Sonja Strykov.

HOBBY. Vicky Marshall.

SALTY. Walter Jones.

GAIL. Who was fifty-seven him!…

HOBBY. Got a beard down here.

*(**HOBBY** gestures to show the beards length.)*

GAIL. I bet he's older than my Dad!

SALTY. And Sasha Rhodes, who had been through nearly all the kids in the school…and some of them, that weren't in the school!

GAIL. They reckon she charges, and she's made that much money, she's having her teeth done!

HOBBY. When they sent you a new teacher, it was like getting some foster parents… When Nixon arrived we were bored and disinterested.

ALL. Nixon's first tutor group!

*(The trio fabricate their tutor group as **HOBBY** becomes **NIXON** once more, with her coat over her arm.)*

NIXON. Hi...Is this Nine.I.B...? I'm Miss. Nixon... It's a bit chilly in here isn't it? Can you two lads come down from the bookshelves, I don't think that they were meant for sitting on, were they? If you don't mind just come down. And if you could stop playing table tennis that would also help. Can everybody sit on a seat and not on a desk? That's better...Right...My name is Miss Nixon.

>(**GAIL** and **SALTY** laugh.)

The entire class burst into laughter. I didn't see that I'd said anything funny. My name is fairly straightforward and I've only got one head. I turned to the blackboard and saw that some joker had drawn some enormous genitals on the board. I looked at the class, they were still laughing. That looks like a penis, I said; only smaller!

>(**HOBBY** puts down Nixon's briefcase and joins **GAIL**.)

GAIL. Oh God!

HOBBY. I don't like her I think she's a twat!

GAIL. I don't like her either.

HOBBY. Same!

GAIL. Same!

SALTY. I do!

HOBBY. Why do you?

SALTY. You've got to give her a chance!

GAIL. Why, do you like her?

SALTY. Yes...and we even gave Miss Bell a chance.

HOBBY. No we didn't.

GAIL. No we didn't!

HOBBY. She's trying to be too smart, I hate teachers who think they're trendy!

SALTY. Yes but she is cool!

GAIL. What do you know about what's trendy Salty!

HOBBY. Yes, you Div!

(LX.)

(A school bell rings. Each actor goes to a desk, as kids. They address the audience as staff, spotlights pick them out behind chairs and or desks.)

WHITHAM. Right quieten down, quieten down, said Maureen Whitham, head of RS, as she pathetically tried to control a class of thirty. Please be quiet. If you don't keep quiet I'll send you to the Reflection Room! Be quiet...Shut up...Now there's consequences coming!

NIXON. As I walked from Lincoln to Ghandi I heard and saw many different types of teaching.

WHITHAM. Please, don't throw the books about, it's one between seven, now everyone be quiet...Right; you're a verbal warning! You're a C One! You're a C Two!

NIXON. It was like being in a human zoo!

WHITHAM. And you're a big fat C you are Oggy Moxon!

*(**SALTY** becomes **MR BASFORD**, donning a nose and glasses combo.)*

BASFORD. Nobody speaks in Dr. Basford's lessons. That's why I have the best maths results in the school. Nobody talks, you can't work and talk, nobody can not even me, and I have a P.hD...amongst many other talents!

NIXON. Most classes had some sort of noise coming from them...

WHITHAM. Right, said Maureen Whitham, as she hopelessly tried to settle her class…A C Three to you, a C Four to you, a C Four Point Five to you! I'm going to get Dr. Basford…Oh… Silence, that's better.

NIXON. Dr.Basford's class, worked in absolute silence, with absolute commitment. He also timetabled that he had the best kids.

BASFORD. Don't let the bastards grind you down, hit 'em low and hard…low and hard, kids respect discipline… If they don't get it at home, they get it in my lessons… Hush down…I can hear someone breathing…

(Physical activity clear the image and sets for the next scene the Main Hall.)

NIXON. I arrived at my first lesson five minutes late, I'd taken a wrong turn at Minghella and found myself in Physics… A year eleven B.Tech Performance Arts group lounged about in the main hall…eleven had managed to turn up. Twenty names were on the register. The school hall looked like a youth club; I walked purposefully to the stage.

*(**NIXON** walks upstage to the desks.)*

GAIL. Oh God it's her, Dixon!

SALTY. Got her for tutor and for drama.

GAIL. What's happened to Mrs Hugill?

SALTY. Left hasn't she?

GAIL. I hate drama. Only did it for a skive.

SALTY. I love drama.

GAIL. Yes but I thought that there'd be no writing, it's nearly all writing!

SALTY. Drama can help you get a job!

GAIL. How can it?

SALTY. Confidence and that! Communication!

GAIL. Got any cigs?

SALTY. Anyway they wouldn't let me do music, said I was too clumsy. I've got two Woodbines, my granny's.

GAIL. Buy a tab off you at break?

(From upstage area, as addressing the entire class.)

NIXON. Get a chair, I said in a friendly, sort of youth worker type of tone.

(The class take no notice.)

GAIL. What's she say?

NIXON. Grab a chair everyone...

GAIL. We're not doing any work, are we, Miss?

NIXON. Can you grab a chair...

GAIL. I'll give you some crisps if I can tab you...

NIXON. Can you all please get a chair and come and sit around the stage in a half-circle...

SALTY. How long have you been smoking?

GAIL. About four months...

SALTY. Why don't you buy some bastard cigs then...

GAIL. I am going to.

SALTY. When?

GAIL. Tomorrow...

NIXON. Can you get a chair and stop waving them around? I know I just said get a chair but I didn't expect you to swing it around your head...

SALTY. If I tab you and you don't bring any cigs I'll slap you...

GAIL. I will, honest…Honest, I will…

> *(Frustratedly.)*

NIXON. Get a chair and sit on the frigging thing!

> *(Slowly taking their chairs to make a semi-circle still nattering.)*

GAIL. What's she say?

SALTY. Dunno.

> *(A beat.)*

NIXON. Will everyone please sit on a bastard chair?

> *(A beat.)*

GAIL. Who's she think she is?

SALTY. Are you going to Maths or are you twagging it?

GAIL. Is she here?

SALTY. Her car's here. It's that red 'un.

GAIL. I'm off into town then, get a milkshake.

> *(Eventually sitting.)*

NIXON. When everyone is ready…Good…I think it would be a good thing for us to start with a very important person in the world of drama. Mr William Shakespeare. And in particular a play that you've probably seen but don't realise it. *Romeo and Juliet*.

> *(**GAIL** and **SALTY** groan.)*

Which is a tragedy.

GAIL. And it's the basis for *West Side Story*, and it's about neighbours arguing.

SALTY. We've done it…

NIXON. Oh right...

SALTY. We did it with Mrs Hugill.

GAIL. And we did about two tramps who're waiting for somebody and he never turns up.

SALTY. And we've done *The Greatest Showman*!

GAIL. And *Hamlet*. About a prince who kills his uncle.

SALTY. And *Blood Brothers!* Good that!

GAIL. And we've done *Shrek!*

SALTY. *Hollyoaks...*

GAIL. What else have we done?

SALTY. *High School Musical.*

GAIL. Yeh. *King Kong*...We've done all that there is in drama Miss!

(**SALTY** *gets to his feet to narrate.*)

SALTY. At that moment, a giant of a lad, Peter Saxon stood up. He must be six feet seven, with tattoos on his arms and a line across his neck which read, "Made in Hull". "I wanna say something", he said, "I've got some drama to tell you..."

NIXON. Go on then, Peter, I said, not knowing what to expect...

(**SALTY** *becomes Pete Saxon, stands as if he is addressing the entire class.*)

SALTY. Right I'm Peter Saxon now...One day, miss, last year, it was great. Me and Tom Wood decided to run away, to seek our fortune. We was going to go to London. It was a Tuesday, I think. But it could have been a Thursday. No, no, it was a Tuesday, cos we had Mr Cooper for Design Technology. Mr Cooper's soft, sir, you can swear at him and all sorts, we used to call him "gibbon head", cos he had a bald head and looked like a gibbon. Anyway, me and Tom are in his class and I throws a chair at him, so he goes and hides himself in a storeroom, so me and Woody lock him in the storeroom, and then we get a chair and stand on it and look at him through the window in the top of the storeroom, and I keeps shouting "gibbon head" to him… Anyway, then we legs it and gets a bus to the station. I couldn't stop laughing, Miss, honest, just the picture of gibbon head sat in that storeroom killed me off. Anyway, Woody says that we've got drama with Mrs Hugill before dinner, so we comes back to do our drama lesson. In drama we did "different visions of hell". I was a cyclops and Woody was my brother-in-law! Anyway, me and Tom got into stacks of trouble. But I liked doing plays when Mrs Hugill was here…When we did *Grease* I loved it! And as far as I know Miss, Mr Cooper is still locked in the storeroom…

GAIL. No he's not you liar…

*(**SALTY** returns to his chair, as **NIXON** addresses the audience.)*

NIXON. They were just natural storytellers; why would you want to knock it out of them? Why don't we celebrate their imaginations? Wouldn't it be more joyous? Yes, they're a funny bunch, but I think they liked me, and I liked them. D'you known what, Whitewall wasn't so bad.

GAIL. Miss? Can we do *Slumdog Millionaire*?

NIXON. Oh that's old school, why don't we do our own TikToks?

GAIL. Do you do TikToks Miss?

NIXON. Yeh, watch! Here we go!

(**NIXON** *launches into a TikTok-style dance. It is clear that she is an accomplished mover. She makes the soundtrack herself.* When she has done it she looks for a response.*)

How about that?

(A beat.)

GAIL. Don't give up the day job!

(A beat.)

ALL. Staffroom, a month later!

(Music.*)

(The stage picture is recreated to suggest the staffroom. Desks are employed with papers and books secreted inside.)

(The Staffroom.)

(LX.)

NIXON. After that first month I was beginning to feel fairly confident. And I also came across; Jackie Prime, PE mistress.

(**PRIME**'s *entrance is significant it is head turning.*)

PRIME. Jackie Prime was tall, sun-tanned, bouncy and an expert at swimming and tennis… She was developing dance in the gym and thought that she was too good for Whitewall, you could tell!

NIXON. Morning!

---

* A licence to produce *Teechers Leavers 22* does not include a performance licence for any third-party or copyrighted music. Licensees should create an original composition or use music in the public domain. For further information, please see the Music and Third-Party Materials Use Note on page iii.

PRIME. Sorry?

NIXON. Nothing I just said, morning!

> *(A beat.)*

PRIME. Are you the new one?

NIXON. I suppose!

PRIME. Q.T. S.?

NIXON. Induction year. it's all a bit new!

> *(A beat.)*

PRIME. Where are you from?

NIXON. Pontefract, but I did a drama degree here at Hull!

PRIME. Loughborough!

NIXON. Okay!

PRIME. Extraordinary place!

> *(A beat.)*

NIXON. And I did an MA at Leeds University so…

> *(**PRIME** doesn't like the academic reference.)*

PRIME. We struggle with the arts in this school.

NIXON. Well I hope to change all that, and Mrs Parry seems supportive.

PRIME. You're like us, on the fringes, they slaughtered Mrs Hugill! The boys want to play rugby and the girls want to get pregnant!

NIXON. Seems like a bit of a generalisation!

PRIME. I've been here ten years!

NIXON. Do you play League or Union?

PRIME. We play Union, we get more fixtures. But some of the lads get signed locally by the Hull clubs.

NIXON. So how did the first fifteen get on, there was a game last night wasn't there?

PRIME. We lost sixty-seven nil.

> (**NIXON** *finds this hilarious and can't help herself.*)

NIXON. What?

> (*A beat.*)

PRIME. That's a good result against St Georges!

NIXON. Is that the private school?

PRIME. They agree to play us once a year!

NIXON. Isn't it a bit dispiriting?

> (*A beat.*)

PRIME. It is but how are they going to learn if they don't play the best?

NIXON. A tough-love policy then!

> (*A beat.*)

PRIME. Well, good luck!

NIXON. Thanks.

PRIME. You might need it!

> (*A beat.*)

NIXON. Like the first fifteen?

> (*It's icy between the two of them.* **SALTY** *becomes* **MRS PARRY**, *with her scarf as she enters the staffroom.*)

PARRY. Morning.

PRIME. Morning, Mrs Parry.

(**PARRY** *comes near* **PRIME** *and* **NIXON**.)

PARRY. Morning Miss Nixon, I hope you're thinking about *The Mikado.*

NIXON. I'm chewing it over.

(*A beat.*)

PARRY. I understand that the first fifteen did rather well Jackie?

PRIME. Very well!

(*A beat.*)

PARRY. Did you know Whitewall has a farm Ms Nixon?

PRIME. Well it's not actually a farm Mrs Parry, we do have a pig.

PARRY. My dear Miss Prime, we have a number of pigs.

PRIME. One's an old sow.

NIXON. And geese?

PARRY. Two geese! Have to go; SLT in five! Then I'm at the other site! Only fifteen miles away, but that's what we get when we're led by donkeys!

(**MRS PARRY** *has breezed out of the staffroom.*)

PRIME. There goes a hundred thousand a year!

NIXON. Really?

PRIME. Makes you think!

(*A beat.*)

NIXON. I was on duty yesterday around the back of the canteen, and I was attacked by one of the geese... But I have discovered how to avoid the smokers, I just look the other way...

PRIME. It's fairly obvious where the kids are going to smoke, and if you want to catch the smokers you can, but it I was you, I wouldn't go behind the Sports Hall...

NIXON. Why's that?

PRIME. That's Oggy Moxon's patch. All the staff leave Oggy well alone.

> (**PRIME** *secrets her baseball cap in the desk. Sits on a desk as* **GAIL**.)

NIXON. And then she left, taking her smirk and fake-tan with her; but I knew that wasn't the last I would see of Jackie Prime!

> (**NIXON** *goes to sit,* **GAIL** *and* **SALTY** (**JONES**) *become two other* **TEACHERS** *in the staffroom, reading and sipping coffee.*)

JONES. You can't sit there, that's Marcus' seat.

NIXON. What about over here?

JONES. That's someone's seat. Andy Collier's.

NIXON. Oh, right. Is this anyone's paper?

WHITHAM. Yes. It's Mr Schmit's, he's on the loo...

NIXON. I can't share a cheek on the edge of that, can I?

JONES. Sorry, no you can't no! I like to be on my own!

> (**NIXON** *moves down stage to address audience.*)

NIXON. Even after seven weeks finding a regular seat in the staffroom was a nightmare. I was told by Leanne Binns that a lot of new staff preferred to stand outside in the rain. Mr Sawyer had been at Whitewall's for two years and not ever got a seat in the staffroom, and the teaching assistants didn't bother going to the staffroom at all; they just hung around the bogs at break times.

> *(**NIXON** moves way upstage, opens an umbrella and signifies being outside on duty.)*

WHITHAM. I do not believe he is doing this. Have you seen the timetable, Basford's gone bananas.

JONES. The man's a pyscho! Always thought that!

WHITHAM. The man does not care, he just doesn't care.

JONES. What's the matter, Maureen?

WHITHAM. I'm on cover in Ghandi for English. I hate that group he knows that I do!

JONES. Oh don't: I've just had Natalie Foreshore in Wilberforce, if that girl says "I'm bored" once again I'll ring her soddin neck.

WHITHAM. But they hate me, he knows they do!

JONES. Do you know what she says… We're looking at the digestive system, and she says, "Miss, the oesophagus is one long tube running from mouth to anus." I said "Very good, how did you find that out?" She says, "Miss, I went to the dentist and he looked in my mouth and he could tell that I'd got diarrhoea." I said, "It's pyorrhoea, girl, pyorrhoea, bleeding gums"…I give up on some of 'em, I really do…

> *(**NIXON** announces from beneath the umbrella upstage.)*

NIXON. There was a big fight at break-time, it was chaos!

(*Music.* **NIXON** dissolves to become **HOBBY** as **GAIL**, **SALTY**, **HOBBY** don beanie hats to become the schools hooligans. They emulate rappers and gangstas as they move downstage in sync, it has the feel of Berkoff meets* West Side Story.)

GAIL. The cock of Whitewall High was Bobby Moxon, known to all and sundry as –

SALTY. – Oggy Moxon.

GAIL. There was no doubt at all that Oggy was dangerous, all the teachers gave him a wide berth.

HOBBY. He was sixteen going on twenty-five, rumour had it that he had lost his virginity when he was ten.

GAIL. And that Miss Prime fancied the pants off him.

HOBBY. When Oggy Moxon said "shit", you did, when he said it was Wednesday, it was Wednesday.

GAIL. What about when he said it was Tuesday?

HOBBY. It was Tuesday!

GAIL. One Tuesday, I was stood outside Marvell, Mr Dean had sent me out because I'd told him that I thought Adolf Hitler was a bossy twat!! And he sent me out… I'm stood there with a mood on when Oggy comes past.

(*LX.*)

(**SALTY** *becomes* **OGGY MOXON**. *An area of stage is illuminated.* **OGGY** *enjoys spitting near to* **GAIL** *as a demonstration of his machismo.*)

---

* A licence to produce *Teechers Leavers 22* does not include a performance licence for any third-party or copyrighted music. Licensees should create an original composition or use music in the public domain. For further information, please see the Music and Third-Party Materials Use Note on page iii.

OGGY. All right, Gail?

GAIL. Yeh.

>   *(To audience.)*

I knew that he fancied me.

OGGY. What you doing?

GAIL. Waiting for Christmas, what's it look like?

OGGY. I'm having a party in my dad's pub, wanna come? Most of the year nine is coming…Should be a good night…

GAIL. Might come then.

OGGY. Might see you there.

GAIL. Might.

OGGY. Wear something that's easy to get off. Your luck might be in.

>   (**OGGY** *spits once more then swaggers upstage.*)

GAIL. I hate him.

HOBBY. Why is he always spitting?

GAIL. Think's he's rock!

HOBBY. Might have a mouth condition!

GAIL. Like what?

HOBBY. Dunno but might have!

GAIL. Somebody ought to drop him.

HOBBY. Who?

GAIL. Couldn't you?

HOBBY. Probably if he started!

GAIL. You're scary!

HOBBY. Am I fuck!

GAIL. See!

HOBBY. What?

GAIL. That's scary!

HOBBY. How is that scary?

GAIL. It just is!

HOBBY. Salty am I scary?

SALTY. Is the Pope a Catholic?

HOBBY. I don't know!

> *(A beat.)*

Anyway all the staff shit themselves when they have to teach Oggy Moxon. Mind you all the staff shit themselves when they have to teach me, so I don't know who's worse!

> *(**GAIL** comes downstage centre. It is her big moment. **HOBBY** goes and watches the speech.)*

GAIL. Right, Oggy's speech about being hard: I'm Oggy Moxon!

HOBBY. We said that you'd have to use your imaginations…

> *(LX spotlight illuminates **GAIL** as **OGGY**.)*

GAIL. I'm Oggy!

HOBBY. It's good this!

GAIL. I'm as hard as nails, as toe-capped boots I'm hard, as marble in a church, as concrete on your head I'm hard. As calculus I'm hard. As learning to drive is hard, then so am I. Even Basford knows I'm rock, if he sticks me in t' Reflection Room I just fiddle with my cock… And if any teachers in the shitpot school with their degrees and bad breath lay a finger on me, God be my judge, I'll have their hides...And if not me, our Nobby will be up to this knowledge college in a flash...All the female flesh fancy me in my "skinnys", no uniform for me never. From big Mrs Grimes to pert Miss Prime I see their eyes flick to my buttonholed flies. And they know like I that no male on this staff could satisfy them like me, cos I'm hard all the time. And as I walk my last two terms through these corridors of sickly books and boredom...I see grown men flinch and fear...In Cookery one day my hands were all covered with sticky paste, and in my haste I asked pretty Miss Bell if she could get for me a hanky from my pockets, of course she would, a student on teaching practice – wanting to help, not knowing my pockets had holes and my underpants were in the wash..."Oh no", she yelped, but in truth got herself a thrill, and has talked of nothing else these last two years... Be warned, when Oggy Moxon is around get out your cigs...And lock up your daughters...

(Music plays. **GAIL** and **SALTY** pick up a chair each they are about to put the chairs on the desks at the end of a lesson. **NIXON** puts on her coat. They buttonhole her, they want to talk. She hangs around, really wanting to be elsewhere.)*

GAIL. Miss, are teachers rich?

NIXON. *(As if in anguish.)* Noooo!

GAIL. What about Mrs Parry, she's got a massive car?

NIXON. She might be, but I'm not.

SALTY. Are you married, Miss?

---

* A licence to produce *Teechers Leavers 22* does not include a performance licence for any third-party or copyrighted music. Licensees should create an original composition or use music in the public domain. For further information, please see the Music and Third-Party Materials Use Note on page iii.

NIXON. *(Another difficult response.)* No. Next question.

SALTY. Got a boyfriend though!

NIXON. Might have!

GAIL. Is he hot?

NIXON. Right, I think this has gone far enough!

> (**SALTY** *and* **GAIL** *try and think of another question which will have the effect of keeping* **NIXON** *talking to them. Meanwhile she picks up his briefcase.*)

GAIL. Miss, is this a school for thickies?

NIXON. Why?

SALTY. Yes coz we failed the Ofsted haven't we?

NIXON. Well...

GAIL. Miss do that dance again!

NIXON. What my TikTok, shall I? Do you dare me? Shall I? Here we go!

> (**NIXON** *gets ready to do the dance once more.*)

You embarrassed?

GAIL. No!

NIXON. You are!

GAIL. Aren't you!

NIXON. I've done worse than that!

GAIL. Oooooh, now we know!

> *(A beat.)*

SALTY. You know like at The Mount School Miss, it says outside; this is a 'good school' and it doesn't say owt like that outside here does it?

(A beat.)

NIXON. Well we'll have to make it a good school won't we?

GAIL. How, by you doing a TikTok?

NIXON. Make sure you do your homework, be on time, get your work in!

(A beat.)

SALTY. Miss I can't finish my work because my phone's broke!

NIXON. Well what's happened to your computer?

SALTY. Haven't got one!

(A beat.)

NIXON. So you're doing your homework on your phone?

GAIL. We all do!

(A beat.)

NIXON. None of you have got computers?

GAIL. Not at home!

NIXON. So you're writing essays on your iPhones?

GAIL. Miss, why isn't drama a core subject?

SALTY. Yes and why is there so much writing, I did it to act not to write!

NIXON. They feel they've got to justify it!

GAIL. Did you do Performing Arts in school Miss?

NIXON. I did but it was different, it was mostly practical, now seventy five percent of B.Tech is written which is crazy!

SALTY. Especially when you're doing it on your phone!

(A beat.)

NIXON. There's computers in school though right?

GAIL. When you can get on them!

> *(A beat.)*

SALTY. I have to go to the bog to work, there's no room in our house!

GAIL. Same, or my Aunty's!

NIXON. My home was like that!

SALTY. Was it?

NIXON. Where do you think I've come from Mars! I go to the supermarket you know!

GAIL. Yes but do you know how much a pint of milk is?

NIXON. Forty-nine pence at Tesco's!

GAIL. Fair!

NIXON. Some students here have got computers haven't they?

SALTY. Some, but not many!

GAIL. Miss, I had one but just played games on it!

> *(A beat.)*

SALTY. Everybody knows that if you come here you're a Div miss!

NIXON. Well you're not a Div are you, and what is a Div anyway, might be just a different way of thinking!

> *(A beat.)*

GAIL. Yes but when we're going home, all the kids from Saint George's ask us if we can add up, and they ask us if we've got any table tennis homework?

SALTY. Miss, all the kids who go to that school are snobs… Their Mam's drive four-by-fours, They're the ones who are burning the planet…

GAIL. Doctors some of 'em, Miss!

SALTY. Yes they send their kids there, drive big cars, and cause more health problems.

NIXON. Which means you're not a Div doesn't it?

(A beat.)

SALTY. Miss because they go there they think they're better than us.

NIXON. They only think it, they might not be! We might think that we're better than them!

(A beat.)

GAIL. Well, they say our teachers are shit. Sorry, didn't mean to say that.

NIXON. Well we might think that about their teachers!

SALTY. Dr. Basford's sons go there, don't they?

NIXON. Do they?

GAIL. Yeh, two twins. "Twinnies" they're called.

(A beat.)

SALTY. Do you like it at this school, Miss?

NIXON. Yeh, it's okay, you lot are awkward, but OK.

GAIL. Miss what do you think it's most important for a teacher to do?

(A beat.)

NIXON. Well, I'm just learning you know, I'm like you, but I think a teacher should have a good relationship, if she hasn't got a relationship she can only ever be a teacher, never a person.

GAIL. What about Dr. Basford, he hasn't got a good relationship with the kids...

NIXON. Well I can't speak for Dr. Basford, can I?

SALTY. Miss the bell's gone...

NIXON. You'd better go and get it then – and go quietly.

> (**SALTY** *and* **GAIL** *disappear upstage slamming the desk tops and shouting loudly.*)

It was a trip to the New Theatre to see *Priscilla Queen of the Dessert* that got me really close to those three, although I had to watch my step they had a habit of getting a bit too close!

> (**SALTY** *becomes* **DR BASFORD**, *and addresses* **NIXON** *from behind a desk upstage, the mood changes dramatically.*)

Dr. Basford you wanted to see me?

BASFORD. Ms Nixon, I understand you took a group of fifteen-year-olds to see a musical play featuring cross-dressing transgender individuals? Now I'm not a prude, but would you mind consulting with me if ever you want to take another trip!

> *(LX.)*

> (**SALTY** *discards* **BASFORD**, **NIXON** *puts down the coat and briefcase to return to* **HOBBY** *and* **GAIL** *joins the narration from chairs and desks.*)

HOBBY. She got a black mark from Basford for that.

GAIL. And that wasn't fair...

HOBBY. Because she paid for the tickets.

SALTY. I didn't know that!

GAIL. It supposed to be a secret?

SALTY. It's not now is it?

(A beat.)

GAIL. In the old days if you had a cover teacher, they had a pink slip.

SALTY. And you'd think, oh no a cover teacher.

HOBBY. I used to think, oh great a cover teacher. We can mess about! They can't really solve problems and that can they?

GAIL. Can't they?

HOBBY. That's what I heard.

SALTY. Yes like we had a bloke who'd been an Engineer in History and he hadn't got a clue.

HOBBY. What, about History or Engineering?

SALTY. Both!

HOBBY. Yes and Dr Basford is in charge of the cover rota right.

*(**GAIL** announces.)*

GAIL. Basford puts Niko on PE cover!

HOBBY. Which was perfect, she could show 'em her TikTok.

*(The three move off their positions with energy to play out the PE cover scene. **GAIL** becomes **JACKIE PRIME** and bounds downstage with a basketball musical sting.)*

(LX.)

PRIME. All right, all year nine deadlegs from Mr Fisher's group shut up, said Miss Jackie Prime. If you want to go and hold the posts for the school cross country go with Mr Clarke's Environmental Studies group. Those who want to do trampoline with me, get changed, you without kit better see Miss. Nixon.

> (**SALTY** and **GAIL** stand in a line across the stage they become the cast off from PE. As they become characters they pull on beans hats or fold scarves around their necks.)

SALTY. A whole line of kids wearing anoraks came forward…Nixon looked staggered, she'd been left to deal with P.E's cast-offs.

GAIL. And amongst the throng was the legendary Barry Wobschall. Barry never did sport.

SALTY. He was fifteen but had the manner of an old man, he lived with his grandad out on the coast and spoke with all the wisdom of someone four times his age. Every day for the past two years he had worked on a milk round.

> (**NIXON** inspects the line, then **SALTY** and **GAIL** change positions, and play all the roles.)

NIXON. Where's your kit?

RON. Miss, my shorts don't fit me.

NIXON. What about you?

PIGGY. Miss, my mother put my shorts in the wash and they got chewed up because the washer has gone all wrong…coz it's connected to the Hive we've just had put in and that's gone wrong!

NIXON. Do you expect me to believe that?

PIGGY. It's true, Miss.

> (**NIXON** moves along the line.)

NIXON. What about you, Barry Wobschall, have you got any kit?

BARRY. No, Miss.

PIGGY. He never brings any kit, Miss.

NIXON. I wasn't asking you, was I, Simon Patterson.

PIGGY. No, Miss.

NIXON. What about a note, Barry? Have you brought a note?

BARRY. Miss.

NIXON. Okay let's have a look at it then.

GAIL. Barry handed him the note. It was small and crumpled. Barry looked on in innocence as Nixon opened the piece of paper.

*(**GAIL** hands **NIXON** a piece of paper.)*

NIXON. *(Reading.)* "Please leave four pints, a pie and a yoghurt this Saturday".

(A beat.)

BARRY. It's the only note I could get, Miss.

NIXON. Really?

BARRY. Yes really!

(A beat.)

NIXON. Fair enough!

(LX.)

(Music.)

*(**GAIL** prepares to be **JACKIE PRIME**, **SALTY** moves to sit upstage. A dappled gobo effect creates the arcadia which is St George's.)*

GAIL. On the thirteenth of October Jackie Prime was at a Safe Guarding event held at Saint George's.

SALTY. As all the delegates came out of the Grand Hall, she was walking around the quadrant, a choir was singing!

*(Amongst the leafy gobo's **PRIME** and **NIXON** meet once more, a choir can be heard singing from the school chapel.*)*

NIXON. Isn't it just amazing?

PRIME. Isn't it!

(A beat.)

NIXON. I would never have guessed it was even here.

PRIME. Our kids call it Hogwarts!

NIXON. I can see why!

(A beat.)

PRIME. Have you seen the facilities, have you seen the pool?

NIXON. Last week I discovered that some of mine are doing essays on their iPhones!

PRIME. They're very generous here with scholarships actually!

(A beat.)

NIXON. You should've seen my school!

PRIME. And mine.

---

* A licence to produce *Teechers Leavers 22* does not include a performance licence for any third-party or copyrighted music. Licensees should create an original composition or use music in the public domain. For further information, please see the Music and Third-Party Materials Use Note on page iii.

NIXON. It was cold and falling to bits.

PRIME. It is here in places!

NIXON. Yes but the difference here is one of the Dad's writes a cheque and it's all sorted.

PRIME. Never judge a book! Cash is in short supply!

NIXON. So there is a God!

>   *(A beat.)*

PRIME. Apparently the Head of Drama here writes for Radio Four.

>   *(A beat.)*

NIXON. Dr. Basford's kids come here did you know that?

>   *(A beat.)*

PRIME. You seem surprised…And Jackie Prime was off, into Saint George's gymnasium.

>   *(**NIXON** stands in the Arcadia which is St George's. She feels the weight of privilege.)*

NIXON. It was fantastic. There was something reassuring about Saint George's that made you want to teach there. To be honest I really wanted to hate it, it was against everything that I'd ever stood for.

>   *(A beat.)*

It was soothing, privileged and academic. The same, I was beginning to think, could not be said about Whitewall.

>   *(LX.)*

(Gangsta beats.*)

(We are at the back of the Sports Hall. **GAIL**, *as* **DENNIS**, *and* **SALTY** *as* **OGGY MOXON**, *are looking at pornography on a phone.)*

DENNIS. Let's have a look?

OGGY. It's disgusting...

DENNIS. Let's have a look my phone's broke!

OGGY. Oggy was streaming some inappropriate content onto his iPhone. For a cig or fifty pence anybody could have a quick look.

GAIL. It was break and Oggy and Dennis are sharing a few cigs and making a mint!

*(***NIXON*** reluctantly comes downstage to the gang.)*

NIXON. What're you doing guys, the bells gone?

OGGY. Nothing!

*(***OGGY*** addresses the audience.)*

I'm Oggy.

NIXON. Well, you're obviously doing something.

OGGY. No we're not.

NIXON. You're not smoking, are you?

DENNIS. No.

OGGY. What if we are?

NIXON. It'll stunt your growth.

---

* A licence to produce *Teechers Leavers 22* does not include a performance licence for any third-party or copyrighted music. Licensees should create an original composition or use music in the public domain. For further information, please see the Music and Third-Party Materials Use Note on page iii.

OGGY. So what?

NIXON. What have you got there?

OGGY. Mi phone!

NIXON. Well the bells gone!

(A beat.)

OGGY. So what, what do you think we are kids?

NIXON. I'm just saying the bells gone!

OGGY. I know I heard you!

(A beat.)

NIXON. I don't want to have to give you a verbal warning!

OGGY. For what?

NIXON. Do you want to just move along?

OGGY. No I don't, I don't want to be here, anyway.

(A beat.)

GAIL. By this time a massive crowd had gathered. And various voices shouted, she's only a drama teacher what does she know about anything?

(A beat.)

NIXON. You know, I think you'd better come with me to see Dr. Basford.

OGGY. He's not going to do anything.

NIXON. Really?

OGGY. Yeh, really.

(A beat.)

NIXON. Well why don't you just move along, what have you got next?

OGGY. Drama Miss I'm going to pretend that I'm a tree?

(A beat.)

NIXON. We don't do that in my lessons!

OGGY. Don't you?

NIXON. No!

(A beat.)

OGGY. It's rubbish mate!

NIXON. Why don't you just…

OGGY. Yes I know, just move along to my lesson, you gunna report me then?

NIXON. Not if you move along!

OGGY. And if I don't?

NIXON. I'm sure you will.

*(**NIXON** steps away from **OGGY** and **DENNIS**.)*

And I turned and walked away, with kids jeering and shouting in the background. And very faintly I heard Oggy Moxon say…

OGGY. You're a wanker Miss!

*(**NIXON** is distressed by these events.)*

(Music underscores.*)

*(LX picks out **NIXON** in a pool of light she is emotional and shook up, she rests on the side of desk. **GAIL** and **SALTY** support the narrative.)*

---

* A licence to produce *Teechers Leavers 22* does not include a performance licence for any third-party or copyrighted music. Licensees should create an original composition or use music in the public domain. For further information, please see the Music and Third-Party Materials Use Note on page iii.

NIXON. I wanted to kick the living shit out of him! But I couldn't deal with Oggy Moxon.

SALTY. Nobody could!

NIXON. And if I couldn't, who I thought was fairly streetwise, what about Mrs Grimes, or Julie Sharpe.

GAIL. Or those nice quiet supply teachers who never have a wrong word for anyone?

NIXON. I'd been in the job for less than four months, and it was wearing me down. The protocol, the marking, the relentless problems, the kids; the lack of ambition, it was just like it was when I was at school, and I wondered if it would always be like that!

> *(LX open state.)*

> *(**GAIL** sat on a desk upstage narrates.)*

GAIL. When Nixon got back, she didn't report Oggy, but she realised that there was a Parent's Evening that night.

SALTY. What she needed was a night round town!

GAIL. What she got was a night sat alone!

> *(A beat.)*

ALL. Nixon's first Parent's Evening!

> *(The trio making a soundtrack of chitter chatter as they set up the stage to represent the Parent's Evening location. They bring a chair to the other side of the stage with the other side facing desk and chair.)*

> *(LX.)*

> *(A spot creates a pool for the scene.)*

NIXON. I'd been sat there for an hour and no one had come.

Maths, Science, even Art had a steady flow. I doodled for a bit, marked some work, then I remembered…

> *(**NIXON** takes a large hairy monster's hand from her briefcase and pulls it onto her hand. She behaves as if she has a false hand, she finds it absurdly funny and she is casually changing position to entertain herself.)*

Don't ask why!

> *(A beat.)*

And guess what? I suddenly had a string of parents turn up.

> *(**NIXON** changes her positions in an attempt to try to hide the hand.)*

It was interesting because no one battered an eye! And just before she left, Hobby's Grandma said; that she hoped I got better soon!

> *(Energy onstage as we get the sense of a very busy corridor. The three of them are caught in spotlights across the stage as they portray various staff members. Anxiety is running high through there staff – **NIXON** has put the monster's hand back into her briefcase, all three of them are looking intensively at their mobile phones as the dialogue is delivered, so they appear to have more interest in their phone lives than their real lives.)*

GAIL. Keep to the left.

SALTY. Keep to the right!

NIXON. Keep to the left and Sanitise!

GAIL. Coming through!

SALTY. One way traffic!

GAIL. Keep to the left

NIXON. Keep to the right!

SALTY. Coming through!

> *(The **TEACHERS** are variously appealing to students in their classes in a strong physical style. The phones go back into their pockets.)*

NIXON. I wasn't talking to you.

SALTY. I was talking to Paul Drewitt,

GAIL. Now will everyone hush down?

NIXON. I shan't say it again.

SALTY. All right, we'll wait till everyone's quiet before we go home.

GAIL. That's a verbal warning!

SALTY. Right you're a C Two! Yes, Yes you are!

ALL. Miss the bells gone!

NIXON. I know the bell's gone, Simon Patterson, and I'm not bothered, I can stay here, all night!

> *(LX.)*

> *(**GAIL**, **HOBBY**, **SALTY** step forward as the spotlight fades and sets up drama club setting.)*

HOBBY. During September we had "drama club" in the school hall after half three.

GAIL. It was brilliant!

HOBBY. I loved it, coz I didn't want to go home anyway!

SALTY. They call it lesson seven.

HOBBY. And in a morning I'd come in early for breakfast. There's nowt at home!

SALTY. I've got a paper round now so I can't get in!

HOBBY. After my Mam left I went to mi Gran's! I don't see owt of him mi Dad!

GAIL. Which is a good thing really isn't it?

HOBBY. Yes, coz he's a right arse!

GAIL. You're lucky you know who your Dad is!

SALTY. Eh?

GAIL. I'm joking!

HOBBY. I liked staying behind, it was like you were special.

SALTY. Yes but sometimes it got a bit awkward, like when we was rehearsing and Mr Franklin, the Head of Maths took a group across the stage.

HOBBY. You should've seen it. Nixon went ballistic. Franklin's like one of the hard teachers but when she saw him go across the stage when we was doing *Blood Brothers* she blew a pipe. Mate she's rock! She's like; how dare you disrespect my work space! And she did that with one of the site staff, didn't she?

(Music.)*

(LX.)

---

* A licence to produce *Teechers Leavers 22* does not include a performance licence for any third-party or copyrighted music. Licensees should create an original composition or use music in the public domain. For further information, please see the Music and Third-Party Materials Use Note on page iii.

*(**HOBBY** becomes **NIXON** and **SALTY** grabs a play script and are beginning to read when **GAIL**, as **DOUG** the caretaker, enters with a large broom, and wearing a High Viz sleeveless jacket.)*

DOUG. Come on let's have you now, times up! Time to go home! I've got this floor to buffer. We might be having to use this for Covid jabs and I don't want it all messing up. And I've got the mobiles to do for night class, and then the sports hall, cos five-a-side's on tonight. And somebody's gone crackers in Ghandi's bogs…

NIXON. Just give us a few more minutes, Doug…

DOUG. A few more minutes? Bloody hell, where would I be if I gave all the staff a few more minutes?

NIXON. Come on, Doug!

DOUG. I'm asking you to leave, that's all.

NIXON. But it's the manner of it…

DOUG. I've got to get this buffered…

NIXON. It's taken me ages to get this lot interested in making their own work – give me another twenty minutes…

DOUG. I can't Missis Nixon… We're short-staffed… I've got three cleaners off with this bloody virus thing they're all talking about!

NIXON. I know isn't it awful?

DOUG. It's gunna get worse from what I've been told. It's gunna be a right mess, if we have to lockdown!

NIXON. Just ten more minutes!

DOUG. I can't there's just me on, Jim's back's playing him up…I'm struggling.

NIXON. We all are!

DOUG. I'm only doing my job.

NIXON. I have one lesson a week to get them interested in my subject. And those that are interested you're wanting to move! How am I going to sensitise them against the Philistines Doug?

DOUG. I don't bloody know!

NIXON. Five minutes?

(A beat.)

DOUG. Look, you don't get paid for this, get yourself off home...

NIXON. I bet you wouldn't get Dr Basford out of his office...

DOUG. You should have a proper room for this drama thing. I mean doing it in the Main Hall is a disgrace... Sometimes I can't get a shine on the floor, I have to polish it...And that's a bloody job.

NIXON. If you can tell me, Doug, where there is any morsel of space for me to do drama I'd be happy to move.

DOUG. Well, it's not worth bloody doing!

NIXON. There isn't anywhere...I've got the Main Hall and that's it. They put my in a Science lab last week, Doug smell the coffee, I'm the lowest of the low, just two minutes! Come on me and you, let's smash the establishment!

(A beat.)

DOUG. Well if you ask me they should take it off, the bloody timetable, I mean, they don't do any writing, make as much noise as they like...

NIXON. That's where you're wrong, they've made it all about written work that's why what we're doing after school is so important!

DOUG. It's a waste of Education Authority's bloody money if you ask me. What are they gunna be, actors? Haven't we got enough?

NIXON. I'm talking about psychologies, I'm talking about interior worlds, I'm actually talking about the use of language and what makes us human!

DOUG. Well I don't know about that!

NIXON. We're the country that gave the world Shakespeare and you're kicking me out for practicing what he made us famous for, think about it!

DOUG. I have thought about it, I want you out!

NIXON. Can't you see what you're doing? Why don't you give us a break you silly old sod?

DOUG. And that's swearing, nobody swears at me, I don't get paid to be bloody well sworn at. Wait till I tell Dr. Basford!

NIXON. Tell him, in fact, I'll tell you what; I'll tell him my-frigging-self!

> (**DOUG** *storms off upstage.* **GAIL** *discards* **DOUG**, *and returns as* **GAIL**, *as if witnessing the scene.* **SALTY** *looks at* **NIXON**.)

ALL. Ooooooh!

SALTY. That was awkward.

GAIL. Why do we get moved all the time?

> (**NIXON** *takes off* **NIXON** *to become* **HOBBY**; *all sense the anxiety as they sit on the desks as they were, they look at the audience things are getting tense.*)

SALTY. Yes, that was an awkward one!

HOBBY. That happened loads!

(A beat.)

SALTY. Never happened in PE did it?

HOBBY. Dunno, I never went!

SALTY. What ever?

HOBBY. Never!

GAIL. What, never ever?

HOBBY. No!

SALTY. What about swimming?

HOBBY. Can't swim, never went!

SALTY. Cross country?

HOBBY. Are you joking?

GAIL. Tennis?

HOBBY. Nope!

GAIL. Netball?

HOBBY. Bollocks to that!

(A beat.)

GAIL. You have never done PE ever in school?

HOBBY. No!

SALTY. How come you're such a unit then?

HOBBY. Dunno, but I have never done PE. I was always ill when we had it!

SALTY. What made you ill?

HOBBY. Having PE!

*(Laughter and energy gets them from their positions as the set up the staffroom **HOBBY** becomes **NIXON**, **SALTY** becomes **BASFORD**. **GAIL** sits as **MAUREEN WHITHAM** on a desk upstage.)*

ALL. November the ninth! Staffroom!

(LX.)

*(**DR. BASFORD** reads The Times Ed. **NIXON** is looking though some marking. She has a plastic coffee cup. **DR BASFORD** has his own mug.)*

BASFORD. I hear that you've had a bit of a run-in with one of the Site Staff.

NIXON. I was going to mention that!

BASFORD. Don't upset them Sharn, they're under a lot pressure with all the rule changes!

NIXON. I know how they feel, I'm not sure when we're supposed to be in or out!

(A beat.)

BASFORD. Well we're doing what we can on Zoom, but it is a mess!

(A beat.)

NIXON. How are they doing things at Saint George's, because I'm not sure many of mine are logging on! Some of them don't have even have computers, they're working on heir phones.

(A beat.)

BASFORD. Fine, as far as I'm aware, they're pretty switched on!

NIXON. Do you live out that way?

BASFORD. No I live down Green Acre Parade.

NIXON. That's this school's catchment area isn't it?

BASFORD. Just on the edge.

(A beat.)

NIXON. So why didn't they come to this school?

(A beat.)

BASFORD. Aha!

NIXON. What?

BASFORD. The old thorny question.

NIXON. That's the Drama Department for you!

(A beat.)

BASFORD. Well St George's gets students into Oxford for a start.

NIXON. So is that what we should all be aiming for?

BASFORD. Chance would be a fine thing!

NIXON. Well if you're talking about the Government.

BASFORD. I wasn't!

NIXON. Not the best examples are they?

(A beat.)

BASFORD. So you're going to bring up, elitism, selection, privilege, hypocrisy, corruption!

NIXON. And networking, unfairness, the establishment looking after itself!

(A beat.)

BASFORD. Look, I'm just making sure that my kids have the best education.

NIXON. And you can afford it.

BASFORD. So will you, one day!

NIXON. If I could afford it I wouldn't do it!

BASFORD. Why?

NIXON. Because it's wrong in so many different ways!

BASFORD. So what am I supposed to do, make my lads disadvantaged because others are? I've worked in the state system for twenty years, I went to a state school. I get it!

NIXON. But kids have a right to a good education regardless of whether their parents have the ability or willingness to choose you know that.

BASFORD. What can I say?

NIXON. You know as well as I do that a lot of parents around here don't attach a great deal of importance to education.

BASFORD. The system is broken, I agree.

NIXON. So surely all schools should be the same, have the same facilities! Shouldn't we want the best for all kids, not just for those whose parents can afford to send them to a good school?

(A beat.)

BASFORD. Of course! And all our food should be the same price; all cars the same price, all our holidays should be the same price, no matter where we go! But that is simply not what we have.

NIXON. I just think that if we banned Private education we would have a fairer society!

(A beat.)

BASFORD. That's never going to happen. With Covid the truth is that the gaps will get wider and wider, most of ours are going AWOL anyway you know that! It'll take years to get them back on track.

NIXON. So that's another reason to ban them!

BASFORD. Well when every socialist MP sends their kids to a state school, I'll send mine!

NIXON. That's been an own goal for years, but all kids deserve the right to be educated to their potential.

BASFORD. And that's the kind of system we have!

NIXON. Well that's bullshit! Examinations are a framework we fit kids into. Look at all the nonsense over Post Codes! Outrageous social stigmatising, what a giveaway that was, you're given an exam result based on where you live! Come on?

> *(A beat.)*

BASFORD. Don't talk to me like that love.

> *(A beat.)*

NIXON. I'm not a love!

> *(A beat.)*

BASFORD. No but, I knew what you were as soon as I saw you.

NIXON. Did you?

> *(A beat.)*

BASFORD. For eight years I've played the main parts in the school productions, eight years!

> *(**BASFORD** leaves the staffroom puts his mask in a desk, and **SALTY** watches the action upstage. **WHITHAM** is distressed by the tension in the staffroom.)*

WHITHAM. "You've had it now," said Maureen Whitham, head of RS, as she sat thumbing through the *Times Ed*. "Basford will make your life a misery, he'll have you on cover from now on till the cows come home. I mean I agree with you but they're his kids!"

NIXON. How can we talk about a fair society if you can pay to buy a better education?

WHITHAM. Well we're all consumers!

NIXON. I know that Maureen.

WHITHAM. I don't think about it, drives you mad. I'm here doing my best for these kids, what else can we do?

NIXON. It's so bloody unfair.

WHITHAM. Nobody said it was ever going to be fair Sharn! It's a shit sandwich. We chose to work here, that's our statement, we can't blame him. We just have to battle on.

NIXON. That's my point!

WHITHAM. What is?

NIXON. It shouldn't be a battle! They've got a theatre, we've not, they've got a swimming pool, we travel to one, they cream off the best kids, we can't! Let them have some of our kids and see how well they do in the leagues tables. The whole hand is rigged!

WHITHAM. I didn't realise it was a competition.

NIXON. It's a competition that they can't lose! I've got to go, I've got a B. Tech year three and we're stuck in Ghandi, if they turn up!

> (**NIXON** *realises she has to be elsewhere. She grabs her briefcase and moves to exit, it is clear that Maureen is feeling the pressure of the job.*)

WHITHAM. I'm supposed to be on cover but I'm not going, I've told him!

NIXON. I can't believe a member of our SLT sends his kids private!

*(**GAIL** dissolves **WHITHAM** and sits on a desk as **SALTY** comes downstage to eyeball the audience. **HOBBY** dissolves **NIXON** and sits on a chair.)*

(LX.)

(Fade the staffroom state.)

SALTY. She told us, that maybe she'd been wrong!

GAIL. That it was alright to have an unfair system.

HOBBY. She said that the whole country seemed happy with that so...

GAIL. We had this discussion about it.

    (A beat.)

SALTY. I mean we've never been to St George's anyway!

GAIL. Never wanted to!

HOBBY. I didn't even know what it wa!

    (A beat.)

SALTY. I just think that t' teachers here are doing their best!

GAIL. Well they got through t' inspection!

SALTY. I mean it was a close thing but they got through it!

    (A beat.)

HOBBY. And Niko was a brilliant tutor, we had her all the way through!

    (A beat.)

SALTY. She kept saying that it's a war!

GAIL. Us, us against the world!

(A beat.)

SALTY. She said we've got to aim high, and if we do and we fail...

GAIL. At least we've had a shot!

(A beat.)

HOBBY. But with Covid it's been chaos. I came in one day and there was only fifteen kids in school!

(A beat.)

GAIL. And when you're feeling down, she always does something daft.

SALTY. Like to cheer the whole class up.

GAIL. She got us doing this thing once!

(A beat.)

SALTY. Shall we do it for 'em?

GAIL. Shall we?

(A beat.)

SALTY. Yeh, come on Hobby!

(A beat.)

HOBBY. Urgh, come on then!

(They nervously come downstage to present themselves.)

Right! Are you ready? After three, right!

One, two, three! Four!

(They perform a very very tightly structured impressive version of Nixon's earlier TikTok dance, which they make the musical soundtrack for themselves. It ends with a huge final flourish, at which they freeze.)

(Blackout.)

(Music*.)

---

* A licence to produce *Teechers Leavers 22* does not include a performance licence for any third-party or copyrighted music. Licensees should create an original composition or use music in the public domain. For further information, please see the Music and Third-Party Materials Use Note on page iii.

ACT TWO

(Christmas time at Whitewall's.)

(The broom is stuck upside down in a upstage desk. Trimmings, a star and a piece of crepe paper adorn the broom, which is now a Christmas tree. **SALTY**, **GAIL** *and* **HOBBY** *take time putting up the tree, and enact their narrative.)*

GAIL. Christmas at Whitewall and love was in the air. All over the school there were Christmas trees and cards and trimmings, and every break time we would queue up to snog Josh Roebuck under some mistletoe in the reference section of the library.

HOBBY. Christmas also saw the culmination of Salty's interest in Ms Nixon.

SALTY. I'm in love with her.

HOBBY. You not.

SALTY. I am, I'm infatuated…

HOBBY. What's it feel like?

SALTY. Brilliant…I was on her table for Christmas dinner…

HOBBY. Yeh but does she love you?

SALTY. Dunno but I'll find out at the Christmas dance…

GAIL. Why, what are you going to do?

SALTY. Snog her…

HOBBY. OOOOOOHHHH, you're not…

SALTY. I'll need some Dutch courage but I am...

HOBBY. I don't believe it...

SALTY. I've got it all worked out. We go to the off-licence, you go in and buy some cider.

HOBBY. Why me?

SALTY. Then I'll bring some spring onions from home. We'll drink the cider then eat the spring onions.

GAIL. Spring onions, why?

SALTY. Because Doug and Mr Hatton will be on the door of the Christmas dance and Mrs Parry says if anyone is suspected of drinking alcohol they won't be allowed in... And I want to make sure I get in.

HOBBY. Are you sure Miss is going to the dance?

SALTY. Course she is, I've asked her a dozen times. I've sent her forty cards in the Christmas post.

HOBBY. Must have cost you a fortune?

SALTY. No my aunty works in a card shop, anyway it's the thought that counts.

HOBBY. So I went into the off-licence, and bought two large bottles of cider.

SALTY. Which we drank through a straw...And then we stuffed ourselves with spring onions.

(Assuming a doorman like position.)

MR HATTON. Bloody hell. Have you been eating spring onions?

*(Referencing **MR HATTON**.)*

HOBBY. That was Mr Hatton's reaction as we came into the disco...

(LX. School disco.)

(Music pulses lowly under.*)

SALTY. Brilliant we're in, I told you it'd work, I'm slightly merry but not out of control.

HOBBY. I feel sick. I hate onions.

*(**GAIL** turns to **SALTY** as if in the disco.)*

SALTY. Gail have you seen Miss?

GAIL. No, is she coming? Brilliant.

HOBBY. Is she here yet?

GAIL. Hey can you smell onions?

HOBBY. Niko hadn't arrived, she was up in the pub with the rest of the staff, and she was sat far away from Dr Basford. Meanwhile down at the disco Mr Dean was doing Chris Moyles impersonations and playing records that were three years out of date...

(Becomes an awful school DJ on the spot. Mixing at a school desk.)

DEANIE. Yes indeedy we're bigging it up in da house with Moose T and da Whitewall massive.

*(**OGGY MOXON**'s presence is palpable.)*

GAIL. Oh shit, look out, Oggy Moxon.

*(**SALTY** becomes **OGGY**, with a sideways worn baseball cap taken from a lift-up desk.)*

OGGY. Got you...

GAIL. Hey oh...great...

---

* A licence to produce *Teechers Leavers 22* does not include a performance licence for any third-party or copyrighted music. Licensees should create an original composition or use music in the public domain. For further information, please see the Music and Third-Party Materials Use Note on page iii.

OGGY. Giz a kiss then...

GAIL. Haven't you got any mistletoe?

OGGY. I don't need mistletoe. Why didn't you come to my party, you owe me one...

GAIL. Later, eh, maybe later...I dashed away from Oggy leaving him wondering what perfume smells like onions...

> *(The trio suddenly begin to dance like they have absolutely no rhythm. Lazzi to bad dancing should bring the house down.)*

HOBBY. It's a fact of life that all teachers dance like retards. They dance like they're all out of a music documentary... It must be the weight of all that knowledge in their heads which makes them look like they're in the back seat of an old Ford Cortina... Mr Dean was a supreme example of bad dancing...

> *(**DEANIE** sings a song in the style of "I'm Too Sexy" by Right Said Fred.*)*
>
> *(He demonstrates extreme bad dancing.)*

HOBBY. Oggy?

> *(**SALTY** becomes **OGGY** and kicks someone in the face. **HOBBY** reacts.)*

There'd been some trouble in the toilets, Oggy Moxon had hit Kev Jones for nothing.

---

* A licence to produce *Teechers Leavers 22* does not include a performance licence for any third-party or copyrighted music. Licensees should create an original composition or use music in the public domain. For further information, please see the Music and Third-Party Materials Use Note on page iii.

GAIL. Kev said that Oggy hit him because he fancied me... Oggy tried to get me to dance but both times I left him and went to the toilets...*(She moves to upstage.)*

*(**HOBBY** picks up Nixon's coat ands briefcase, from upstage and 'enters' the disco.)*

NIXON. Simon Patterson, very smart...Merry Christmas.

GAIL. Merry Christmas, Miss...

NIXON. Where's Salty?

GAIL. Dancing. Hobby's in the loo... Have you been drinking?

NIXON. Only a pint, I'm in my new car.

GAIL. Yeh you need a car when you're drinking and driving.

*(**NIXON** steps forward and addresses the audience.)*

NIXON. The Christmas dance had all the seriousness of a big disco, and the fifteen and sixteen-year-olds looked stunning. At a quarter to ten Deanie played the last record, a smoocher and Salty appeared in front of me and suddenly my face was confronted by the strong smell of onion...

*(**HOBBY**, as **NIXON** and **SALTY** smooch. **GAIL**, as **OGGY MOXON**, hangs around.)*

SALTY. It was fantastic...

*(**NIXON** still has the briefcase while smooching.)*

NIXON. It felt a bit awkward to be honest.

*(**GAIL** narrates.)*

GAIL. Mrs Parry looked on, she felt a mixture of jealousy and condemnation. But it wasn't unknown for teachers to dance with students especially at Christmas.

SALTY. Doug the caretaker cleared the dance floor in a few minutes. And just as I was going to kiss Miss, she turned her head to wish Doug –

NIXON. *(Turning her head.)* – a Merry Christmas, Doug...

GAIL. Oggy Moxon had seen Salty and Niko dancing but he left the hall in silence...

SALTY. Miss said that she would give me a lift down home, Gail and Hobby decided to walk it home and maybe get a pizza...

> *(Two chairs are positioned centre stage to become the car.)*

NIXON. I got into my car, a twelve-plate Fiat Five Hundred, and Salty jumped in beside me, and before I knew it, into the back jumped Oggy Moxon...

> *(LX special creates the car.)*

> *(**SALTY** and **NIXON** occupy the front seats **GAIL** becomes **OGGY MOXON** behind them.)*

OGGY. Oh yeh, what's going on in here then?

NIXON. Will you get out, Oggy?

OGGY. Will you get out, Oggy? No I will not.

NIXON. Get out.

OGGY. No, let's go a ride, eh...? Drop me down home, will you?

NIXON. Get out.

OGGY. Make me.

NIXON. Get out...

OGGY. Make me…

NIXON. I shan't say it again…

OGGY. I shan't say it again. Come on, Miss, make me get out…

NIXON. This is my car, I'm not in school hours, now get out…

SALTY. Come on, Oggy…It's not fair.

OGGY. What's not fair? You want me to go so that you can have Miss all to yourself?

NIXON. I'm going to get Mrs Parry…

OGGY. What the fuck is she going to do about it?

NIXON. Will you get bloody out…

OGGY. You make me…

NIXON. Arrgh…

> (**NIXON** *hits* **OGGY** *in the face in slow motion by actioning an outrageous head butt. Both parties are in agony and holding their heads they get out of the car. Screaming.* **OGGY** *pulls himself out of the car.*)
>
> (*LX loses the car ands favours night time scene.*)

OGGY. You've broke my nose, you bastard…

SALTY. Miss!!!

OGGY. You bastard…

HOBBY. There was blood everywhere…

GAIL. I was screaming, Nixon was shaking.

SALTY. A few members of staff came running from the school…

(**HOBBY** *discards Nixon's jackets during narration.*)

HOBBY. Oggy staggered away from the car. (*As* **OGGY**.) Our Nobby'll get you Nixon… Wait till next term our Nobby'll hammer you. (*Pause.*) And he was off into the dark. It was like a film… Everyone was shouting and trying to calm things…And in the distance you could hear Oggy Moxon shouting…"I'm gonna do you, Nixon. I'm gonna do you…"

GAIL. As we stood, a boy ran past us and jumped into his father's car…And a voice bellowed out…

SALTY. Stop running, Simon Patterson!

(*LX.*)

(*Music.**)

(*Blackout. After a pause the lights come up again, and the trio are sat on the desks and chairs looking at the audience. What they have just demonstrated was a fantasy. It wasn't their experience.*)

I loved Christmas!

GAIL. Yes but, that's not what happened to us!

HOBBY. Sound's good though…especially the head butt! That wa' sick!

(*A beat.*)

SALTY. There's been no Christmas parties for us…

GAIL. …not for two years.

---

* A licence to produce *Teechers Leavers 22* does not include a performance licence for any third-party or copyrighted music. Licensees should create an original composition or use music in the public domain. For further information, please see the Music and Third-Party Materials Use Note on page iii.

SALTY. We haven't had any parties in school.

GAIL. "No parties of any kind!"

SALTY. That's what Mrs Parry said!

HOBBY. Unless you're Boris Johnson.

GAIL. She didn't say that!

HOBBY. I bet she wanted to!

(A beat.)

SALTY. And I missed 'em to be right!

GAIL. I didn't, coz you don't miss what you've never had!

SALTY. Idiot!

(A beat.)

HOBBY. But lockdown was hard to be fair.

SALTY. Tell me about it!

GAIL. I was like just stuck in my bedroom!

(The atmosphere is serious.)

SALTY. Everybody was!

HOBBY. Some of our mates haven't ever come back!

SALTY. True dat!

GAIL. I've not seen Seb Jackson for a year!

HOBBY. Somebody said he'd had a breakdown, couldn't handle it, gone psychotic or sommat. Mental health and that.

GAIL. Shocking.

SALTY. I mean we've all be the same haven't we but...

(A beat.)

GAIL. Anyway...

HOBBY. Yes...

> *(A beat.)*

GAIL. You couldn't get a lift from a teacher now,

SALTY. Or dance with 'em.

HOBBY. Yes like when I heard about that I thought "what?"

> *(A beat.)*

SALTY. Teacher's can't be your friend now.

GAIL. But they want to know if there's owt wrong like, you know if you're suffering from abuse or owt.

HOBBY. Gail?

GAIL. It's true.

SALTY. Or like if there's drugs, or radicalisation.

HOBBY. Safe guarding and that!

GAIL. There's staff for it!

> *(A beat.)*

HOBBY. I suppose it's good all that, but I would have preferred the old days when you could just head butt a bully in the face, know what I mean. Sick that!

SALTY. That was made up you nugget!

HOBBY. Was it?

GAIL. Yes, she would have lost her job mate!

HOBBY. Still sick though!

> *(**HOBBY** mimes the head-butt herself.)*

Bang get down!

> *(A beat, and then a sudden burst of energy.)*

ALL. New Year 2022!

    (LX.)

    (Picks out the staff in three spotlights as they become the staff. **SALTY** *as* **PARRY**, **GAIL** *as* **WHITHAM**. **NIXON** *is stage centre.)*

PARRY. Morning, Sharn.

NIXON. Morning, Mrs Parry.

WHITHAM. Happy New Year!

PARRY. Happy New Year!

NIXON. Happy New Year!

    (A beat.)

WHITHAM. Had a nice Christmas?

NIXON. No not really.

WITHAM. Same.

PARRY. Same!

    (A beat.)

WHITHAM. Glad to be back?

NIXON. No not really!

PARRY. Same!

WHITHAM. Same!

    (A beat.)

PARRY. Do anything nice?

WHITHAM. We went for a walk!

PARRY. So did we!

NIXON. Same!

WHITHAM. Same!

>   *(A beat.)*

PARRY. Do anything for the New Year?

NIXON. Went for a walk!

WHITHAM. Same!

PARRY. Same!

>   *(A beat.)*

You'll never guess what?

WHITHAM. Go on.

PARRY. Jackie Prime got married, to Colin Short!

WHITHAM. Head of PE from Saint George's?

PARRY. Did it over Christmas.

WHITHAM. I didn't know…

PARRY. Neither did I…

NIXON. She'll be going there next!

PARRY. No, she's Whitewall through and through!

WHITHAM. I'd never go there!

PARRY. Nor me!

NIXON. Same!

WHITHAM. Same a thousand times over!

PARRY. Same to the power of R!

NIXON. Yes same!

PARRY. Oh and don't forget your targets!

(Music underscores. **WHITHAM** and **PARRY** hold a freeze as **NIXON** speaks to the audience from her bedsit.)*

NIXON. Whitewall was aiming for Specialist Technology status so if it missed its targets...I was teaching drama one lesson a week! There'd been talk of a drama-room, but Jackie Prime told me there'd been talk for five years! The pressure was unrelenting, but the thing keeping me going was the kids.

(LX.)

(Music fades away.)

*(The Main Hall **NIXON** becomes **HOBBY**, as the trio become youths and animated once more.)*

GAIL. During January it was freezing in the Main Hall!

HOBBY. I think they'd turned t' bastard heating off or sommat!

GAIL. Must be the cutbacks!

HOBBY. What cutbacks?

GAIL. I don't know but there's cutbacks all over!

*(**SALTY** is enthused.)*

SALTY. One lesson in drama though right, Miss asked us to do some work about classroom control and awkward students, so we came up with this scene right!

GAIL. Oh it was sick!

---

* A licence to produce *Teechers Leavers 22* does not include a performance licence for any third-party or copyrighted music. Licensees should create an original composition or use music in the public domain. For further information, please see the Music and Third-Party Materials Use Note on page iii.

(The trio begin to set up the scene.)

HOBBY. In the staffroom there's a red phone, like a batphone, and it glows really red when someone's on the other line.

GAIL. And in each classroom under the desk there's a buzzer, so if a teacher gets into some trouble or has a kid who is getting stroppy they can either give them a verbal warning.

SALTY. And C One or C Two!

GAIL. Or they can press this buzzer, and the phone rings.

*(**HOBBY** imagines picking up the phone.)*

HOBBY. Bring, bring!

*(**SALTY** paints the scenario.)*

SALTY. Right, in the staffroom, just like sat about all day drinking coffee, and reading ancient books are these Japanese martial arts experts, who are trained to kill kids,with karate chops or sharp stars that they throw. And in the staffroom are a number of wires, so that these Avengers –

HOBBY. – when they get the call –

SALTY. – can jump out of the window of the staffroom and be at the root of the problem in a few seconds…

(They display the scene.)

GAIL. Right I'm the French student, and I'm teaching…

HOBBY. I'm Rachael Steele – and I throw something at the board.

GAIL. *(With a French accent.)* Zut alors! Who was that… Who was that who was throwing missiles towards my head? This is very dangerous and could be if someone gets hurt… Was it you, Rachael?

HOBBY. What, miss?

GAIL. You know what?

HOBBY. No I don't, you silly gett...

> (**GAIL** *is incensed.* **SALTY** *pulls an nylon tight legging over his face.*)

GAIL. And then suddenly the French student presses the buzzer for insolence.

SALTY. The phone rings...

HOBBY. The Avengers are in action... Out of the staffroom window, coffee all over the place...

GAIL. Five seconds later...They arrive, kick the door down, tear gas all over the place...

> (**SALTY** *becomes a Marvel Avenger hero, with kicks and smoke bombs, kung fu kata's and the like, with a huge sword which is clearly a prop from* The Mikado *and slices Rachel in to pieces, blood spurts all over from her, her throat is cut. The students love the gore of this modern* Titus Andronicus.*)*

HOBBY. The teacher had a mask secreted in her desk.

GAIL. Merci...

SALTY. Coment Ca Va!

GAIL. The French student is back at work...Un, dieu, trois...

> (**HOBBY** *transforms from Rachel to the School Head making a phone call.*)

HOBBY. A call is made to Mr and Mrs Steele, would they like to come and collect the remains of their daughter Rachael from the school morgue. She was killed during a French lesson. Thank you...

(SALTY and GAIL present for a bow as HOBBY becomes NIXON.)

GAIL & SALTY. The end!

SALTY. The Avenger was played by Salty!

GAIL. And Gail Saunders was the French assistant!

SALTY. This was a Salty Gail Production for Netflix!

(NIXON is disarmed by their efforts.)

NIXON. It was stories like that, which kept me alive at Whitewall. And the kids grew in confidence and their imagination knew no bounds…

GAIL. You can't teach imagination, can you, Miss?

NIXON. I don't know, you tell me.

GAIL. When was the battle of Hastings?

NIXON. Ten sixty-six.

GAIL. What can you do with a brick?

NIXON. Eh?

GAIL. What can you do with a brick? I saw this in a magazine…

NIXON. Build a house…

GAIL. Yeh and…?

NIXON. Throw it.

GAIL. That shows the violent side of you. You can do unlimited things with a brick. You can drill a hole in it and wear it around your neck… You could marry a brick…

SALTY. My cousin married a prick!

GAIL. There's lots of different answers. It says in this magazine that you can exercise your imagination, that's what we do in drama.

SALTY. And art...

GAIL. Yes but you can't choose both can you?

SALTY. You have to choose either drama, art or music Miss! What if you're interested in all three?

NIXON. You can't be interested in all three, the Government won't let you! Unless you go to a private school then you can do what you like!

SALTY. I might write to my MP Miss!

GAIL. Who is our MP?

SALTY. Dunno; have we got one?

GAIL. Miss in most lessons we're like robots. Who invaded England in ten sixty-six? Arm up, Norman the Conqueror, easy mate!

SALTY. Bells gone!

GAIL. Leg it!

(LX.)

*(**SALTY** and **GAIL** run upstage to the desk base making a racket. **NIXON** downstage.)*

NIXON. On January the twenty-first Mrs Parry called me to her office. She said it was urgent. Drama had been made a core subject, I knew it!

*(**SALTY** becomes **MRS PARRY** with the help of her scarf. We are in her office.)*

PARRY. Sharn thank God you're here!

NIXON. Is what I said to Dr Basford?

PARRY. I'm afraid it's worse!

NIXON. We failed the Ofsted?

PARRY. Have we?

NIXON. I don't know I thought you were in charge!

PARRY. I don't even know which site I'm on!

NIXON. The Secretary of State for Education's not visiting is he?

PARRY. No it's not that bad!

NIXON. Amen to that!

(A beat.)

PARRY. Can you do Koko? Mr Gill, who had the part slipped a disc last night building the set. Can you step into the breach? I'd regard it as a great personal favour?

NIXON. Yes, I, well, I am a female and the casting is normally…

PARRY. It's absolutely fine, be a new spin!

NIXON. I have agreed to be in the chorus…

PARRY. You can do that as well, someone as good as you; can't you?…

*(**NIXON** steps out of the scene and plays to the audience.)*

NIXON. And so it was that Mrs Parry got me to play Koko.

PARRY. Wonderful, wonderful, we rehearse Wednesdays and Sunday…See you Sunday.

GAIL. When Dr Basford heard the news he went barmy with the cover rota.

NIXON. And for the next three weeks, I was on cover all the time, Modern Foreign Languages, Design Technology and Open Heart Surgery!

(Music.*)

(LX.)

(The Mikado rehearsals, a dreadful soundtrack of a poor version of The Mikado *plays under.** **MRS PARRY** *directs towards the audience.* **GAIL** *becomes* **DOUG** *and* **NIXON** *looks at the stage/which is the audience at the car crash of a production.)*

PARRY. Pick your teeth up darling… Just pick them up and keep singing… Move left, dear, no, left! There's no need to slouch in the chorus Dr. Basford, you are gentlemen of Japan, not lepers.

NIXON. The primary school students were so cute.

PARRY. Teeth and smiles!

NIXON. Mrs Parry's production before Covid was *Bugsy Malone*, it had lasted six and a half hours… This could be longer!

DOUG. Face t' front!

PARRY. Stay on stage, don't come out and watch!… It's no good saying "I was just coming to watch this bit", stay on stage!

NIXON. The whole thing was a car crash!

PARRY. Carry on!

NIXON. But for Mrs Parry it was close enough for jazz.

PARRY. Never work with animals, children and amateurs.

NIXON. I know what you're saying.

---

* A licence to produce *Teechers Leavers* does not include a performance licence for any third-party or copyrighted music. Licensees should create an original composition or use music in the public domain. For further information, please see the Music and Third-Party Materials Use Note on page iii.

PARRY. Do you know your lines?

NIXON. Yes.

PARRY. Oh that's interesting!

NIXON. Would you like me to get up and join the…?

PARRY. Oh no, if you know your lines you needn't bother coming till the dress rehearsal! Okay where's the Mikado, where's Pooh-bah, where's Nanky Poo?

DOUG. They're in the Music room doing a Wordle.

PARRY. Well tell them that I need them NOW!

*(**DOUG** moves upstage and shouts loudly.)*

DOUG. Oi come on here, you're bloody on…

*(**PARRY** evaporates into **SALTY** at the desks upstage. **DOUG** comes downstage and **NIXON** moves downstage, they counter point each other to the audience.)*

(Musical sting.)

(LX.)

NIXON. During January the Main Hall was used as a Covid-19 Booster centre.

DOUG. …Well we've all got to do uz bit!

NIXON. So I was put in a Food Tech room.

DOUG. …You're lucky there was one free!

NIXON. During February the mock exams were in there!

DOUG. That's what we're here for!

NIXON. So I was in a Child Development room!

DOUG. It's all about targets!

NIXON. Then I had five days in Ghandi!

DOUG. I could have put 'em in the gym but PE asked me not to!

NIXON. Then two days in the front office.

DOUG. And it's cold in the sports hall!

NIXON. I thought about teaching in the back room of the Zoological!

DOUG. I'll give her Drama!

NIXON. And I was on the school field for a week, but Jackie Prime said, we were too noisy!

> (**SALTY** *brings energy to proceedings and all set up the next scene.*)

ALL. March 2022. Tutor group!

> (*Musical sting.*)

> (*The class scream and create their tutor group.* **DOUG** *and* **NIXON** *are rested and* **HOBBY** *and* **GAIL** *sit and rock on desks and chairs.* **SALTY** *picks up a brochure for St George's from inside a desk upstage and brings it to* **HOBBY** *and* **GAIL**.)

> (*LX. The Tutor Group classroom, venetian blind gobos create ambiance.*)

SALTY. Have you seen this?

GAIL. What is it?

SALTY. Brochure or somat for that St George's thing.

> (*A beat.*)

GAIL. What's that doing?

SALTY. Dunno, it was on Miss' desk!

> (*A beat.*)

HOBBY. ' she got that for?

SALTY. Dunno, but it looks posh!

> *(A beat.)*

HOBBY. Do we have one of them brochures then?

SALTY. Never seen it!

HOBBY. S'have a look.

> *(**SALTY** passes the brochure to **HOBBY**, and she starts to finger her way through it.)*

God!

GAIL. What?

HOBBY. Swimming Pool! Cricket nets! Big Library, massive! Theatre!

> *(A beat.)*

SALTY. They've got a theatre at Archies!

GAIL. And Kingswood!

SALTY. And Wyke!

GAIL. And St Mary's

SALTY. Got a brilliant theatre; our Laura did "Wyke's Got Talent"!

> *(**HOBBY** is engrossed in the brochure and reads on flicking the pages over.)*

HOBBY. It says this is professionally run!

> *(A beat.)*

Oh God!

GAIL. What?

HOBBY. Oh what?

GAIL. What?

> *(A beat.)*

HOBBY. Stuff you can do!

GAIL. What?

HOBBY. Chamber Choir!

GAIL. Not for me!

> *(Reading.)*

HOBBY. String En…sem…En…sem bal, whatever that is.

SALTY. Orchestra!

> *(Reading.)*

HOBBY. Oh God!

GAIL. What?

> *(A beat.)*

HOBBY. Cooking for University!

GAIL. What?

HOBBY. That's what it says!

> *(A beat.)*

GAIL. Who wants to do that?

SALTY. People who're hungry!

HOBBY. Who are going to University!

GAIL. Why don't they just learn when they get there?

> (**HOBBY** *is still reading.*)

HOBBY. Ju Jitsu. Wrestling! Parkour!

SALTY. What?

GAIL. What's Parkour?

SALTY. Jumping about!

(A beat.)

HOBBY. Mindfulness!

GAIL. Stop it!

HOBBY. That's what it says here!

GAIL. You can study Mindfulness?

SALTY. Fucking hell!

(A beat.)

GAIL. Do they do Motor Vehicle Technology?

(A beat.)

HOBBY. Doesn't say so!

*(**HOBBY** closes the brochure.)*

I've got to go, I've got a dental appointment.

*(**HOBBY** stirs from her seat.)*

GAIL. Better put it back, so she doesn't know we've been looking at it!

SALTY. What do you think she's got it for?

HOBBY. Dunno, But I wouldn't go there, looks like it's full o' twats!

(A beat.)

SALTY. It's full o' twats here!

GAIL. Yes, us!

*(**HOBBY** puts the brochures back in a desk upstage.)*

HOBBY. See you tomorrow.

(**HOBBY** *exits upstage to become* **NIXON**.)

GAIL. What we got next?

SALTY. Drama, haven't we?

(*A beat.*)

GAIL. How are we gunna work in our group if she's at dentist?

SALTY. Where are we?

GAIL. Dunno but we're not in t' Hall!

SALTY. Why?

GAIL. Roof's leaking!

SALTY. What about that room in Plater?

GAIL. Can't go in coz they used the wrong glue to stick t' tiles down and it's toxic!

SALTY. What about t' coal bunker?

(*A beat.*)

GAIL. What's she got that brochure thing for then, do you think?

(**NIXON** *and enters from upstage.*)

NIXON. Right guys! Maths room!

GAIL & SALTY. Urghhhhh Miss!

(*A beat.*)

NIXON. Oh it feels a bit gloomy in here, is everything alright?

(*A beat.*)

GAIL. Yeh, Miss a hundred percent!

(**SALTY** *tries to inject energy but there is something hanging over them. They reconfigure the space.*)

SALTY. So we go to this Maths room right?

GAIL. And we're on the top floor of Brady!

SALTY. And we're reading this play called *The Marat Sade*.

GAIL. Which is about Asylums!

SALTY. And revolution!

GAIL. Anyway guess who's got an Maths class in the next room!

(*A beat.*)

SALTY. Honestly, you couldn't make it up!

(*A beat.*)

ALL. Dr Basford is a Basford!

(**NIXON** *watches* **GAIL** *walking like Charlotte Corday who is a sleep walker, and reciting lines from the* Marat Sade *is a off-kilter crazy fashion.* **NIXON** *loves it. She moans loudly and woefully.* **SALTY** *is involved then moves upstage to put on a mask which denotes* **DR BASFORD**.)

(*LX, A different type of classroom.*)

(**BASFORD** *is furious as he enters the classroom.*)

BASFORD. Miss Nixon, can I ask you to keep the noise down? I've got a High Flyers group next door and we can't hear ourselves think.

NIXON. I'm sorry!

BASFORD. It's like bedlam in here!

NIXON. Yeh great, isn't it? They've really taken to it. We're doing the *Marat Sade*.

(**BASFORD** *yells.*)

BASFORD. Quiet!

NIXON. Easy!

(**GAIL** *is in fear,* **NIXON** *is astonished.*)

BASFORD. Keep the noise down!

NIXON. Hang on!

(*A beat.*)

BASFORD. It's like a flaming riot.

NIXON. They're enjoying themselves.

BASFORD. Enjoying themselves?

NIXON. Exactly!

BASFORD. That level of noise is not acceptable!

(*A beat.*)

NIXON. Well they're looking at one of the most difficult plays of the twentieth century.

BASFORD. Really?

NIXON. Yes, really!

(*A beat.*)

BASFORD. Sounds like mayhem!

NIXON. It's set in Charenton, the Asylum, and it's a good example of Artaud's Theatre of Cruelty!

BASFORD. You're telling me! Sounds like they're screaming to get out of your lesson!

(*A beat.*)

NIXON. I bet there's more High Flyers screaming to get out of yours!

BASFORD. What did you say?

NIXON. I said that I bet there are more students screaming to get out of yours!

(A beat.)

BASFORD. How dare you?

NIXON. I bet they are bored to death to be honest!

(A beat.)

BASFORD. I need to have a word with you young lady!

NIXON. Young Lady, how patronising is that?

(A beat.)

BASFORD. What?

NIXON. I'm not taking that from a middle-aged white man!

(A beat.)

BASFORD. I have never been so insulted in my life!

NIXON. Oh come on, you must have been, a man like you!

(A beat.)

BASFORD. My students are not bored!

NIXON. Well they certainly look it! You could've heard a pin drop as we came passed I thought they were all dead!

(A beat.)

BASFORD. I want a word with you in my office at break time if you wouldn't mind Miss Nixon!

(**BASFORD** *looks daggers at* **NIXON** *who slowly leaves in silence.* **SALTY** *puts the* **BASFORD** *mask in the desk upstage.* **GAIL** *goes to sit on a desk and listens to* **NIXON** *speak to the audience.*)

(Silence.)

NIXON. He was pissed off!

(**SALTY** *from upstage.*)

SALTY. Why though?

NIXON. Because I'd got an interview at St George's.

(A beat.)

GAIL. I knew there was sommat!

(**NIXON** *continues addressing the audience.*)

NIXON. According to Mr Shaw he had applied for the Head at Saint George's job and had not had his references taken up, and he'd never get over it!

(LX.)

(Music. Choral.*)

(Saint George's Private School. **SALTY** *and* **GAIL** *become the St George's interview staff, two rather old and very posh trustees.* **NIXON** *positions a seat with her back to the audience as she goes through the end of of the interview process.)*

---

* A licence to produce *Teechers Leavers 22* does not include a performance licence for any third-party or copyrighted music. Licensees should create an original composition or use music in the public domain. For further information, please see the Music and Third-Party Materials Use Note on page iii.

(A large window gobo of an old hall picks out the three actors.)

MS COATES. Well thank you very much, Miss Nixon, it's been a pleasure talking to you.

MR CLIFTON. We're sorry to lose Mr Gunther, but he wants to be a playwright and he is leaving to give it a go, as they say!

MS COATES. Obviously we have other candidates to see but we should be able to let you know either way before Easter.

(To audience.)

MR CLIFTON. Her interview at Saint George's had gone very well.

MS COATES. Very well.

MR CLIFTON. Mr Clifton, one of the governors of Saint George's thought she would be outstanding.

MS COATES. Outstanding

MR CLIFTON. He also thought she would be a marvellous asset to Saint George's Amateur Players, a society run by Mr Clifton.

*(**CLIFTON** and **COATES** dissolve, as light fade on them. **NIXON** turns in her seat to speak to the audience.)*

(LX.)

NIXON. Saint George's was a sanctuary compared with Whitewall, kids stood up when a teacher went into a class, no one leaped for the door when the bell rang. Not only did they have a theatre, they had a purpose built studio, with a budget donated by a former pupil! It almost made me cry!

(A beat.)

I was told that the Site Staff often sat in and watched drama classes, and not one single person had ever walked through a drama lesson!

(LX.)

(Music.)

(A choir sings*. Then the singing is drowned out by a track in the style of Dr Dre's music, as the energy shifts and we are back around the tennis courts at Whitewall. A double desk is positioned centrally with two chair on top of it and the narrators play the scene from behind and through the chairs as is they have their faces up against the wire of the tennis courts.)

GAIL. One Wednesday when not a lot was happening Jackie Prime had organised a tennis competition. Some of us were allowed out on to the courts.

SALTY. You mean court!

GAIL. Whitewall only had one decent court. The rest were like dirt tracks.

SALTY. Miss had been invited to take part at the last minute because Sue Edwards had a meeting with the Social Services.

HOBBY. Forty-love, game Prime. Hard luck, Miss Thorn.

GAIL. Miss Thorn got thrashed and so she took her class back to the mobiles to study the Cold War, she was a bad loser.

---

* A licence to produce *Teechers Leavers 22* does not include a performance licence for any third-party or copyrighted music. Licensees should create an original composition or use music in the public domain. For further information, please see the Music and Third-Party Materials Use Note on page iii.

HOBBY. Forty-love, game Prime. Bad luck, Mrs Fish, you've got bowlegs. You should've gone to sea!

GAIL. Jackie Prime was an ace tennis player, somebody said she'd been a county player as a kid!

SALTY. Niko had no kit, she looked like Barry Wobschall. She borrowed a pair of pumps from big Ann Saxon and some shorts... Somehow, mysteriously, she got a bye into the final. And in the final played Jackie Prime!

HOBBY. Yes, would you believe it?

SALTY. When Niko came on to the court all the kids were laughing.

(They laugh.)

HOBBY. Are you sure you know what you're doing Miss?

SALTY. All the kids had their faces pushed against the wire of the courts.

(They pull a face with their hands to show this.)

GAIL. Go on, Miss Prime smash the ball through her head. That was Oggy Moxon!

HOBBY. Forty-love.

GAIL. Smash her Miss Prime!

HOBBY. Game Prime!

GAIL. Dr Basford was smirking the sort of smirk that only Drs can do.

HOBBY. Game Prime!

GAIL. Come on, Miss Prime smash her...Shouted Oggy, like a wild animal...

SALTY. And she tried to...It was like watching Christians in the Colosseum...

*(**PRIME** and **NIXON** step forward either side of the central chairs and desks, they have a tennis racquet and begin to physicalise the game making the noise of the ball bouncing.)*

NIXON. Love all.

*(**NIXON** bounces the ball then serves, the rally is astonishingly long and a direct copy from Wimbledon. The effort from the two women is exceptional, at the end of a very long rally **NIXON** wins a points. **SALTY** cheers.)*

SALTY. Fifteen-love…Well done, Miss, you've won a point. I didn't know you could play?

*(**NIXON** steps forward nonchalantly.)*

NIXON. Yeh, what they didn't know, what none of the staff knew was that I was an under-nineteen tennis international…And I thrashed Jackie Prime. One-six, six-love, six-love.

GAIL. Jacke Prime left the courts in haste. All the kids looked gob-smacked.

NIXON. I could have spared her of course, but I thought; bollocks why should I?

*(**NIXON** replaces the tennis racket to become **HOBBY**.)*

ALL. Niko! Niko! Niko!

*(**SALTY**, **GAIL** and **HOBBY** are thoroughly energised by this memory.)*

HOBBY. With the end of term only six weeks off Niko had this idea of me, Gail and Salty doing our B Tech presentation that we did on Zoom for the leavers!

SALTY. It was hard work because we had to fit it around all our other exams.

GAIL. Yes, and there was no where to rehearse obvs!

HOBBY. Salty was buzzing!

SALTY. I was running around school like a headless chicken. I'd even written in spray paint on the side of the Wilberforce

GAIL. – Dr. Basford is a sad Basford.

HOBBY. All the staff thought it was amusing. Basford didn't, he put Salty on a long list of leavers who had to see Mrs Parry...

>*(LX.)*

>*(**HOBBY** becomes **MRS PARRY** with the scarf for the first time. The trio reconfigure for Mrs Parry's office. A gobo of a window picks her out and **SALTY** who stands begin a chair in her office.)*

PARRY. You don't come to school to fool about, to waste your time. We treat you like young adults and we expect you to behave accordingly. I don't think that writing silly words on a wall is a mature thing to do. Do you?

SALTY. No, Mrs Parry.

PARRY. Well why did you do it?

SALTY. Fed up, Mrs Parry.

PARRY. Fed up of what? What are you fed up of?

SALTY. Loads of things, Mrs Parry. Covid! My mental health! Where I live! Our Laura's boyfriend! How long have you got!

PARRY. Well we are living through very challenging times, but that doesn't mean we can afford to go off the rails.

SALTY. Yeh but Mrs Parry, out there, there's just a load of lies. Where's the truth? Why do we have to do one thing, when other people can do something else? Why are people being judged how clever they are, on where they live?

PARRY. Well you've obviously been having some very interesting discussions in tutor group!

SALTY. And we only know what we know, how much is going on to put us down that we don't know?

PARRY. Well...

SALTY. And why isn't it fairer, why can't we have what they've got at St George's? Just because we haven't got the money!

PARRY. Well...

SALTY. Do you think that's right?

PARRY. Well...

SALTY. It's not right!

PARRY. Well Building Schools For The Future has pumped a lot of money into the City!

SALTY. And it's still not a level playing field, you know it's not.

PARRY. Well that's as...

SALTY. Why can't we do drama, art and music in this school, aren't we good enough? Aren't we sophisticated enough? Are we only supposed to be interested in core subjects? Who's idea was that? And why isn't drama a core subject, we gave the world Shakespeare Miss. Or is it because drama makes you question stuff? And nobody wants people to question stuff do they?

PARRY. Just one second...

SALTY. I'll tell you what the problem is...it's Politicians... them men on the telly with funny haircuts, who talk about choice and equality and fairness...Why don't any of them live on our estate?

PARRY. Well...

SALTY. Why don't they come into this school? I've never seen any of them down the welfare hall or at t'Bingo? Do they even know how much a pint milk is? They say they represent us, but they don't live here. They don't even send their kids to school here.

PARRY. There is really no need to raise your voice to me!

SALTY. They're not bothered mate, they just want to get on the Tele…It's just a game, most of them don't care, and what's worse, they're not even bothered that they don't care.

    (**SALTY** *turns to the audience.*)

Then I turned and left her room!

    (**PARRY** *is moved, frustrated and angry.*)

PARRY. We are doing our best here, do you hear that? We are doing our best!

    (*Musical sting.*)

    (*LX.*)

    (*The Staffroom is created in a pool of light centre stage. There is a real sense of relief amongst the staff.*)

WHITHAM. Congratulations. You did it.

JONES. Well done, Sharn.

WHITHAM. When do you start?

NIXON. September.

JONES. Nobody stays in teaching these days! Nobody! Too bloody hard that's why!

WHITHAM. We'll have a drink after *The Mikado*, said Maureen Whitham, who was playing Sing Sing. I've got a job in the Prison Service, make it a double celebration.

*(**NIXON** turns and with some regrets addresses the audience.)*

NIXON. That was me out of there; and it was then when I realised that Dr Basford is really a hero!

JONES. I've got another interview, it's my seventeenth this month.

WHITHAM. Orrrr...

(A beat.)

ALL. The opening night of *The Mikado*!

(LX.)

*(We are now onstage for a post show audience address. **NIXON** and **GAIL** are upstage **SALTY** dons the scarf and comes downstage centre in a slight spot over a general state to speak to the* Mikado *audience.)*

PARRY. Thank you, thank you, all for coming. It's been a very difficult time and I'd like to thank you all for supporting the school. The Primary school students were wonderful and I know that their parents will feel very confident about sending them to our school. We live in a world full of choices and what choice could be better than Whitewall?

PARRY. I'd also like to take this opportunity to inform you that we have had a 'good' Ofsted report which is a wonderful testament to our inspiring staff and students, many of whom will leave us shortly and progress to either Wyke, Bishop Burton or Wilberforce, and we wish them well on their educational journeys!

NIXON. It was the shortest production of *The Mikado* in history, fifty-five minutes. Forty-six pages of the libretto had been skipped over.

PARRY. And I'd like to thank Simon and Peter for numbering the chairs.

NIXON. The "thank yous" went on for three hours.

PARRY. And Joyce, Chloe and Francis who did the little buns and cakes, and how lovely they were as well.

NIXON. Some of the cast went home!

PARRY. And Jatinder and Chris for cutting the squares of cinemoid which made all those lovely colours. And to Desmond and Sue who helped park the cars. Thanks to you all.

> (As **PARRY** *dissolves upstage* **GAIL** *comes down stage and becomes* **DR BASFORD**. *LX focus centre stage.*)

GAIL. On the last night of *The Mikado* Mrs Parry threw a party on the stage. Everyone chatted and drank Pomagne from paper cups. Dr Basford was there.

> (*As* **DR BASFORD**.)

So, I suppose it's congratulations, Miss Nixon?

NIXON. Sorry?

BASFORD. Congratulations. You must feel very pleased with yourself?

NIXON. Not really.

BASFORD. You were a very good Koko, it was quite a swan-song.

NIXON. Thanks very much, Dr Basford!

> (*A beat.*)

BASFORD. I'm sure you'll have a great time over at Saint George's. It's what you want, isn't it? They're quite into drama over there. The twins are thinking of drama at A-level, good for confidence isn't it? This is not a school for drama, never has been!

NIXON. I think every school should be a school with drama at it's heart Dr Basford!

BASFORD. That's as maybe!

NIXON. I guess!

BASFORD. You just have a thought for us, still stuck here. Mind you, every cloud has a silver lining as they say, Mrs Parry has just asked me if I'd like to play Nathan Detroit in next term's *Guys and Dolls*.

NIXON. And are you?

> (*As* **BASFORD** *makes his way upstage.*)

BASFORD. My dear, the part was made for me!

> (**BASFORD** *takes himself upstage and dissolves, there is an inevitable sense of ending falling across the trio.*)

HOBBY. All the kids were really sad when Nixon left, and me and Salty and Gail all cried.

GAIL. We never saw her again. Somebody told us she was having a good time at Saint George's, and that all the posh kids loved her.

> (*LX.*)

> (*A school bell rings. End of school. The lights slowly change.* **SALTY**, **GAIL** *and* **HOBBY** *are lost. They move around the stage slowly, and pick up their bags. They are full of emotion as they face new sixth form futures.*)

GAIL. Oh well... So that's it then!

HOBBY. The end.

SALTY. Miss, can I just say before we go, don't leave. The kids here need teachers like you!

GAIL. Miss, if you stay, we'll come back and bug you. We'll let you know how we're getting on. I'll come and cut your hair if you like... I'm going Hull College, doing Hair and Beauty, want to do makeup! Miss there's a theatre!

SALTY. I'm going to Wyke, Miss I want to go to Salford and do drama like you said!

(Close to tears.)

GAIL. Don't leave, Miss...

(A beat.)

HOBBY. I'm doing Public Services at Bishop Burton, bet I hate it.

(A beat.)

SALTY. If you stay here we'll come back and do another play.

HOBBY. Best thing I've ever done at school this...

SALTY. We could have a laugh, start a group up.

GAIL. And rehearse at nights...

SALTY. Hey we could do all sorts...*Marat Sade*.

GAIL. Comedies.

HOBBY. Tragedies.

GAIL. Westerns.

SALTY. Kung fu...

GAIL. Miss, romances...

HOBBY. Sex plays Miss, that'd be good...

SALTY. Why don't you do *The Mikado* Miss...?

GAIL. Miss, you said that was shit.

(A beat.)

HOBBY. Anyway...See you...See you, Mrs Hudson...

(A beat.)

SALTY. Yeh. Thanks Miss...

GAIL. Yeh.

SALTY. Yeh.

GAIL. Thanks a lot.

SALTY. See you...

(A beat.)

HOBBY. Yeh have a good un; but you know what Miss, you're a liar!

(She had agreed not to make it personal.)

GAIL. Hobby?

SALTY. Leave it!

HOBBY. After all you've said: you're just a liar mate!

*(**MS NIXON** has changed her mind and is going to stay in their school and not go to St George's. Lights fade to black as music plays*.*

(Lights fade to black.)

Curtain

---

* A licence to produce *Teechers Leavers 22* does not include a performance licence for any third-party or copyrighted music. Licensees should create an original composition or use music in the public domain. For further information, please see the Music and Third-Party Materials Use Note on page iii.

www.ingramcontent.com/pod-product-compliance
Ingram Content Group UK Ltd.
Pitfield, Milton Keynes, MK11 3LW, UK
UKHW021839210426
5322IPUK00022B/376